The Ones Who Believed

TRUE INSPIRATIONAL STORIES HONORING
EVERYDAY PEOPLE WHO TOOK A CHANCE,
SHAPED A LIFE AND MADE A DIFFERENCE

Karen Lopez McWilliams
and
Mary Lou Kayser

Copyright © 2016 by Karen Lopez McWilliams.

All rights reserved. No part of this publication may be reproduced, distributed or transmitted in any form or by any means, including photocopying, recording, or other electronic or mechanical methods, without the prior written permission of the publisher, except in the case of brief quotations embodied in critical reviews and certain other noncommercial uses permitted by copyright law. For permission requests, write to the publisher, addressed "Attention: Permissions Coordinator," at the address below.

Karen Lopez McWilliams/KLM ARCH COMPANY, LLC

1540 Keller Parkway

Suite 108-312

Keller, TX 74628

www.oneswhobelieved.com

Graphic Design by Yevhen Chuhuievets

Cover Design by The Kingfisher Group

Ordering Information:

Quantity sales. Special discounts are available on quantity purchases by corporations, associations, and others. For details, contact the "Special Sales Department" at the address above.

In certain stories, names have been changed to protect individual privacy.

The Ones Who Believed/ Karen Lopez McWilliams. —1st ed.

ISBN-13: 978-0-9982341-0-6

Dedication

THE ONES WHO BELIEVED is dedicated to my husband and soulmate of 28 years, Chalmer Close McWilliams III. Thank you for always believing in me and supporting my goals and dreams. Your friendship, partnership and love completes me. I love you.

This book is also dedicated to all of the everyday champions in this world who believe in others and change lives.

When I give the best of me, that becomes my legacy.

—KAREN LOPEZ MCWILLIAMS

Acknowledgments

"None of us is as good as all of us."

Ray Kroc, founder of McDonald's

There are a host of people I want to thank because I know I wouldn't be who I am today without their impact on my life.

Dr. John W. Andrews, Ph.D.
Vice President – Accreditation and Licensing, Zenith Education Group, Inc.
Because you believed in me as a college student, I began to believe in myself.

Mary Lou Kayser, M.A.T.
Author and Writing Consultant
Thank you for supporting my vision from day one! Your style of writing nobly represents both the storytellers and their honorees. Thank you for making this all possible.

Dr. Jayne Gardner, Ph.D.
Life Coach
Not only do you see the best in people, but you also see their unlimited potential. Thank you for challenging me to step into the light.

To our dedicated and loyal business management staff for their strong leadership and focus on the day-to-day operations. You have allowed me the time and energy to chase a dream, complete a passion project, and write a book.

To my awesome parents, John and Pat Lopez, for being the best parents a daughter could hope for!

To my amazing children, Chalmer and Diana. I am the luckiest mom in the world. Thank you for your love, respect and friendship.

Again, thank you to my husband and best friend, Chalmer!

To my "sister friend," Jana McWilliams. I am so lucky to have a friend like you. You are definitely a "rippler" and have had long-lasting impact on so many lives!

Dr. Tamara Miller
You are not only a talented professional but also a guardian angel to so many.

Joseph Hughes and the Ryan Wayne team
For asking the difficult question and showing me the way back.

Dr. Bill Dorfman
For passing on the currency of confidence to me at key points during this project.

Renee Wilson Simas
Editor and Proofreader
For your eagle eye and exceptional line editing skills, along with your insights in the final stages of the manuscript's production, thank you.

To each of the storytellers in this book, thank you for your time, your generous spirit, and for believing in this project. I couldn't have done it without you! My deepest gratitude to: Brad Ball, Lisa Deer, Dr. Bill Dorfman, John Lee Dumas, Jim Estrada, Nicole Gibson, Eddie Gossage, Bibop Gresta, Dr. Robin Hall, Robert Hayman, Tristan James, Debbie Johnston, Katherine Jones, Mary Lou Kayser, Mark Lack, John Lopez, Bryant McKeon, Ben Osorio, Melissa Nickelson, Krista Dabakis Price, Johnny Rutherford, Newy Scruggs, and Julia Telligman.

Contents

Introduction: The Ripple Effect 1

The Tap on the Shoulder by Karen Lopez McWilliams 9
    Honoring John Andrews

Walking toward Greatness by Tristan James 15
    Honoring Donald Hitt

The Collie Factor by Brad Ball 23
    Honoring Bob "Collie" Colombatto

The Currency of Confidence by Dr. Bill Dorfman 31
    Honoring Barbara Dorfman

The Measuring Stick by Melissa Nickelson 39
    Honoring Mrs. Rita Palm

A Package Combo by Mark Lack 47
    Honoring Craig and Sandy Lack

A Soft Landing by Debbie Johnston 55
    Honoring Richard Johnston and Buddy Allen

Nothing but the Best by Robert Hayman 63
    Honoring Fred J. Hayman and Emil Sziraki

The Noble Mentor by Ben Osorio 71
    Honoring Dean Franklin

"We Did It, Pop!" by Johnny Rutherford 79
    Honoring John Sherman Rutherford, Jr.

The Ride through Two Worlds by Krista Dabakis Price 87
    Honoring Shirley Palmer

The Revelation by Katherine Jones 91
    Honoring the One Within

Family First by John Lopez 99
    Honoring Victor and Connie Lopez, and Herman Gallegos
A Medical Love Story by Dr. Robin Hall 109
    Honoring Dr. James R. Hall
Three Little Words by Bryant McKeon 117
    Honoring Jim "Jimbo" McGhee
Behind Closed Doors by Nicole Gibson 123
    Honoring Sherry Kelly
Success Has Many Parents by Jim Estrada 131
    Honoring Raymond and Julia Estrada
The Power of Impact by Newy Scruggs 139
    Honoring Educators and Role Models
A Pioneer's Legacy by Lisa Deer 147
    Honoring Dr. Linda Holloway
A Man of Few Words by Julia Telligman 155
    Honoring Robert Howery
The Power of Learning by John Lee Dumas 159
    Honoring Benjamin Franklin
The Golden Thesaurus by Mary Lou Kayser 167
    Honoring Robert "Bob" Feinstein
A Different Path to Success by Bibop Gresta 173
    Honoring Mentors of Innovative and Disruptive Thinking
One Hot Night by Eddie Gossage 181
    Honoring Howell Lee "HL" Gossage and Bruton Smith
Bronko, a Symbol of Love by Karen Lopez McWilliams 191
    A Daughter's Story Dedicated to Her Parents
My Final Thoughts and A Call to Action 197
Call to Action Tools 201
Now It's Your Turn 203
The Ones Who Believed Questionnaires 205
Sample Note of Thanks 215
Mentoring's Powerful Legacy 217
Afterword 225

An Invitation from Karen Lopez McWilliams 227
Helpful Internet Resources 229
Key Questions for Group Discussion 231
Key Questions for Personal Reflection 233
Contributor Profiles 237
To Learn More about OWB Contributors 245
About the Authors 247

Introduction
The Ripple Effect

Dear Reader,

Not long ago, I was sitting at my desk one afternoon reflecting on my life. Happily married with two children and a thriving business, I found myself remembering my college adviser, John Andrews, and the profound influence he'd had on me during a particularly challenging time during that season of my life. Encouraging me to reach for a goal I had not considered possible, he caused me to believe in myself in a way that would ultimately affect who I've become and the life I now enjoy. In this moment of reflection, I realized how deep and wide the impression he made on my life truly was. A strong desire came over me to let him know how much I appreciated him for believing in me all those years ago. I wanted to thank him and share details of how his belief has impacted my life. After a quick search, I found him online and sent him a message. But for some reason, it didn't seem like it was enough. I wanted more.

The question was, how?

Fast forward to today. My life coach, Dr. Jayne Gardner, challenged me to do something that I've always wanted to do. I could've chosen any number of things, but for my stretch goal, I picked writing a book honoring everyday champions who believe in others like John Andrews had believed in me. I had a hunch that many people had a story about someone like this from some point in their lives. I wanted to follow that hunch and see where it led. What began as a passion project quickly evolved into much more than I ever expected, providing insights into the profound effect that guidance, influence, mentoring and belief can have on our lives.

The idea for the structure of this book came to me one night while talking to my dad. My parents were hosting a family BBQ, and we were relaxed, sharing a good bottle of wine and listening to music. One of my dad's favorite songs has always been "My Way" by Frank Sinatra, a song written by Paul Anka for what was to be Sinatra's swansong. The song is about a man reflecting on his life experiences. The powerful voice and soaring melody has struck a chord with millions of people worldwide as they reflect on their legacies. While my dad's reasons for liking that song are his own, the lyrics describe a life well-lived by a person who is confident, determined, and grateful – a man like my dad. I grew curious about who had influenced him in his abundant life.

I asked him, *If there was one person who positively impacted, made a difference, and influenced you, who would it be and why?*

What happened next was magical.

I watched as his face relaxed and his mind went to another time. He became noticeably peaceful and happy as he began to tell me his story in vivid detail. The person he spoke about clearly shaped him into the great individual and businessman he is today. The experience of seeing him transform right before my eyes inspired me, and I thought, *I need to write his story down.*

About a month later, my husband and I were vacationing with some friends. I decided to ask my friend the same question I'd asked my dad. To my delight, I saw the same transformation happen to him as the one I'd witnessed in my dad. Watching him open up and smile as he remembered the man who believed in him before he believed in himself made me smile, too. It was the same reaction that I had when I remembered John Andrews. Later it occurred to me that, as they both shared their stories, I had witnessed their deepest gratitude flow through their body language, eyes, words, and facial expressions.

This is great, I thought. *I'm definitely onto something.* Turns out, my hunch was accurate: everyone has a story. In a world of seven billion people, there are a lot of "ones" who believe, and for some people, there is truly just one. They are everyday heroes who help others elicit their best self and forge a new path in life, one they may never have imagined or considered.

The more I thought about the nature of the "ones who believe," the more I saw how closely it mirrors what happens when a pebble is dropped into a pond. The exchange of potential and kinetic energy that results when the weight of the pebble hits the water produces and reproduces the ripple, and is known in the scientific world as "the ripple effect." This energy continues to spread outward in a series of circles to the shore until we can no longer see its effects. But it doesn't end there; the ripples then return to the source where the pebble initially entered the water.

The energy set forth from our actions and the actions of others is just like this, and is a powerful force. Ripples are about energy and movement. Even the smallest pebble causes a ripple, and this energy never ceases to exist, even if we can no longer see the ripples on the water's surface. I was inspired. *Couldn't the ripple effect apply to human experience, as well?* I wondered. *After all, wasn't John Andrews' belief in me and the way my life has turned out essentially a manifestation of the ripple effect?*

When I applied the concept to my father's story, and then to my friend's, it worked for them as well. Out of this test, I created a name for this specific kind of person, what I call a "rippler."

Essentially, a rippler is *someone who effects a positive change in another's life that has far-reaching and long-lasting impact.*

The idea for this book began to take shape and gain clarity.

I teamed up with writing consultant and author Mary Lou Kayser to help me bring the concept to life. First, I developed a set of questions I wanted to ask the people I would interview for the book. At the center of those questions was the one I'd started with when talking to my dad and my friend. I then created a list of people I wanted to interview.

This book is the culmination of those interviews, a ripple effect in its own right. I talked first with people in my inner circle of influence, followed by many interviews with people in the ever-widening ring of ripples that naturally occurred through referrals. Their ages range from teenagers to senior citizens. I was honored to talk with each one of them, as their backgrounds and life experiences were as varied as their ages. Students, entrepreneurs, corporate executives, supervisors, life coaches, media personalities, moms, dads, and one three-time winner of the Indianapolis 500 are but some of the stories you will read. Their stories are deep, real, sometimes sad, and often intense. As I listened to each story, I was moved that people would let me into their most personal space to understand the significance of the one(s) who believed in them.

When I first began this project, I expected to hear my interviewees identify and talk about one special person who had believed in them, someone who played an important role in shaping who they are today. What I wasn't prepared for was how difficult it was for some people to pick just one person to honor.

For example, when I spoke with Dr. Bill Dorfman, aka the "Celebrity Dentist," he said, "It's very rare to find everything in one mentor, but it is possible to have one consistent force throughout your life. The one person who believes in you no matter what." Similarly, when I listened to Jim

Estrada's story, he pointed out, "Success has many parents." This pattern showed itself time and time again with each new interview, bringing to light the universal connection between belief and success. The connection was revealing. Most of the storytellers have unknowingly cloned some of their honoree's characteristics in their professional or private lives, sometimes both, and have become ripplers in their own right.

During the interview process, I noticed that people enjoyed hitting the pause button on their busy lives to take the time to fondly remember their special memories of ones who believed in them. One of the patterns I noticed when I had the chance to meet with my interviewees face to face was how quickly we lost track of time. Some of my conversations could have lasted for hours! Even the conversations I had over Skype allowed my interviewees to step back from their everyday lives and reflect on fond memories and the people who inspired them.

There were so many ah-ha moments for me as the book evolved. One detail in particular became clear: the roles we play in life are critically important. A mother's or father's love, a grandparent's presence, a business mentor's support, a spouse's love and encouragement, a legend's wisdom or an educator's engagement. The unexpected notion that another person simply believes in you causes a feeling that never goes away. Perhaps this is why the positive memory is so powerful and often transfers into their own behavior.

I learned something else from these stories: when others believe in you during your life, you learn to believe in yourself. That belief gives you the permission you need or needed to awaken to your own potential. The cycle continues when you find yourself believing in your kids, your grandkids, your family, your coworkers, or your students. Indeed, it is the power of the ripple at its best.

In a culture that tends to focus more often on the negative than the positive, we need stories like the ones in this book. These stories serve as a bridge to bring us closer together instead of driving us further apart. As John C. Maxwell points out in his book *Intentional Living*, "Stories are how we relate to others, learn, and remember. The telling of our stories becomes an emotional connecting point for us. It bridges the gap between us." By giving a voice to ordinary people who are committed to an extraordinary responsibility -- influencing and shaping the lives of others in a positive way -- I'm able to pass on my own desire to make the world a better place.

Introduction The Ripple Effect

This book also provides tremendous insights for anyone working with people in an advisor or mentoring capacity -- at work, school, or in a family. It can inspire leaders in these settings to ask questions, start conversations, and strengthen bonds that make people connect and feel closer. It is, after all, the relationships in life that matter most. The revelations about these organic relationships, mentorship and the roles mentors play in our lives inspired me to include a special section entitled *Mentoring's Powerful Legacy*. Although it comes at the end of the book, I invite you to read this compilation at any time and return to it as often as you feel inclined. You will find a list of questions and tools there that will help you bring these conversations to life.

At the end of the day, this book is about personal connections, those genuine relationships that catapult us into action and purpose. It will inspire you to remember those who impacted your life in a positive way. It will lead you to make your own ripples, complete the circle and send the most powerful gifts you can give – expressing your gratitude, and passing on the legacy of the human spirit.

You will discover that not one of the people featured in this collection gave their time and energy for their own glory, but from a place of genuine service and belief in making a difference to others and then passing it on. I wanted to honor these "ripplers" through the voices of the people whose lives they shaped, impacted, and influenced as a way of showing how far simple acts of belief and assurance can go.

When I accepted Dr. Gardner's challenge to do something that I've always wanted to do, I had to muster every ounce of belief in myself that I possessed (and draw on my closest believers) to achieve the goal of writing this book. What I've discovered on this journey celebrating the ones who believed is that I also want to take gratitude to the next level and engage as many people as possible to join me in making ripples in the pond of humanity.

I once read that stories are a light switch to action. By telling these true stories, my goal is to create an emotional connection that inspires you to remember ones who influenced, shaped, and impacted your life. Should showing gratitude and appreciation become part of our everyday life objectives? I think so! Wouldn't it be amazing to launch a consciously positive movement that honors and celebrates everyday champions like the ones featured in the stories in this book? What a gift to thank and express gratitude to those who lifted you up and shaped your life! I've even provided tools you can use to do just that at the end of this book, including a template for a letter of gratitude for those readers who would like help getting started

In addition to showing your gratitude to those who have believed in you, I also hope you will walk away with a desire to become a rippler in your own right within your own circle of influence. In our busy world, it is too easy to miss living in the moment and seeing the needs of others. If your eyes are closed, it is my hope they will open to the potential in yourself and others. The power of belief is the pebble dropped in still water. It is my wish that the ripple becomes a wave, and the wave a rising tide.

Together, we can make a splash that's heard around the world and change lives one believer at a time. Let's make a difference together. Will you join me? I sure hope so. Let's go!

Karen

Karen Lopez McWilliams
November 2016

Just as ripples spread out when a single pebble is dropped into water, the actions of individuals can have far-reaching effects.

— DALAI LAMA

The Tap on the Shoulder

by Karen Lopez McWilliams

Honoring John Andrews

It was a warm day in September 1982 when I stepped onto the campus of Citrus Community College for the first time. A wide-eyed 18-year-old, I was both nervous and excited for a new start. My parents had moved our family to California for their business the summer before I started high school, and those first four years in the Golden State had been little more than a blur. I discovered college presented new opportunities for me. I was looking forward to what my next chapter had in store.

Once I got my schedule figured out, I joined a few clubs on campus, knowing that would be a good way to meet people and make new friends. It wasn't long before I became a student representative for one of the clubs, and it was through that experience when I first met John Andrews. Little did I know how much of an influence and impact he would have on me and my life.

John was the Director of Student Affairs at Citrus Community College. He was tall, warm, and always had a genuine smile on his face. His generosity, sense of humor, and approachable personality made him popular with and well-respected by students and colleagues alike. He loved his job and worked hard to make the college experience good for everyone.

One day late in the spring semester, after a student government board meeting, John gave me the proverbial **tap on the shoulder** and asked if he could meet with me for a few minutes.

"Of course," I said, without hesitation. I'd been in my role as a student representative for about a year. It didn't seem unusual for a meeting.

When I sat down across from him in his office, John leaned back in his chair.

"Have you considered running for student body president?" he asked.

Surprised and flattered at the same time, I shook my head. "No, I haven't."

"Well, Karen, I think you'd be really good at it. There will be a lot of work, but I think you'd be a good leader and I know we would work well together. You ought to consider it!"

I was in shock, but I also remember smiling from the inside out. John was encouraging me to run for student body president! He wouldn't have suggested I run for this important role if he didn't believe in me. And if he believed in me, I knew I could do it. As I reflect on that moment, it was the first time I began to believe in myself!

I immediately told my best friends Laura, Diane, Peter and Chalmer that I was going to run for office. They offered to support me any way they could.

The campaign ran for about five weeks. We had a student forum, created flyers, and I spoke to a lot of students and faculty during the time leading up to election day. Many of my friends helped me during this time. Little did I know one of those friends would become my soulmate. I ran and won---and five years later Chalmer and I would be married. In fact, John was in our wedding. To this day, he and my husband remain in touch.

I remember calling my parents to tell them the good news about winning the election. They were in Washington D.C. with my brothers. I could hear the excitement in their voices! Their daughter was beginning to spread her wings.

Coming from a large family, I didn't have a sense of personal self yet; so much was always going on. I always knew I was part of a large, loving family. This was, by far, my foundation, but I just hadn't discovered who I was yet. With John's belief and support, my new-found friends and independence, I was introduced to the person inside me waiting to be released!

The leadership role as student body president opened doors for me I never imagined. During my tenure, I worked with many of the college's administrators as well as the College President, Dr. Dan Angel. I felt valued and respected by everyone. I was eventually appointed as a Student Representative on the Board of Trustees, which exposed me to professional business leaders, different management styles, budget discussions, and how these decisions affected students' college experience and the cost of education. All of these experiences would prove useful to me in my future careers.

One of John's gifts as a leader was creating a community in the student government program that felt like being part of an extended family. I felt welcome from the very beginning, which I now understand is one of the most important jobs a leader of any organization has. His leadership style was like a magnet pulling me in. I could relate to and identify with his leadership style, which is one of the many reasons I thrived in his presence. He was also skilled at working with every personality type, another leadership quality I have come to appreciate and embrace in my own work today running our company.

John modeled other important leadership skills as well. When any of us on the student government needed help working through personal family issues or stress, his door was always open. I can't tell you how many times he helped me and my cohorts take a deep breath, see the big picture, and formulate a plan to get through whatever happened to be troubling us at the time. He never judged, and he was always willing to listen.

While he created a positive, high-functioning environment, John also kept a bull's-eye focus on the work we needed to get done. Because of his inclusive leadership style, no one felt alienated. We all dedicated many hours to completing the tasks and service projects for the greater good of the college and extended community. When John needed to make a point, however, his familiar smile would transform before our eyes into an intense, exaggerated stare. When he tilted his head and walked away with long strides and hands in his pockets -- what we affectionately dubbed the "John Walk" -- no one questioned what needed to happen next. He made his point and we knew what to do.

After leaving Citrus with my degree, the leadership experiences I had under my belt prepared me for immediate roles in the community including working as the American Heart Association Special Events Specialist alongside Magic Johnson and his team on the first Magic Johnson Golf Classic. I also worked directly with the chairman of the event, John C. Argue. I knew this was an important role because Mr. Argue was a highly respected attorney in Los Angeles. I was excited and ready to work professionally with these volunteers because of my exposure and mentoring with influential leaders in college.

While working at AHA, I was assigned to be a liaison with significant philanthropic financial donors. For one of the projects, I had the pleasure of talking to Bill Bixby, Burt Lancaster and other high-end private donors. As one might imagine, I was elated to hear their distinct voices on the other end of the phone when they called my office. I also was in charge of organizing private research tours showing our big donors how their money was being used for research and to fight heart disease.

About ten years ago, I was reflecting on the many blessings of my life. I recognized how much John had impacted the direction I took and the decisions I made to have the bountiful life I now enjoy. Today, my husband Chalmer and I are business owners in Texas. I am also a Certified Life Coach for the Mindset for Success program, helping people in my spare time who could use extra support during challenging periods in their lives.

I decided to find him on Facebook and let him know. Once I shared my gratitude with him, I felt complete. I have a strong hunch that many of my college friends would want to thank John for influencing them, too. This is why he gets the very first stamp of approval with #OWB.

Thanking John made me curious about how many other people out there have had a John Andrews in their lives. My passion project was born. At its core, "The Ones Who Believed" champions everyday heroes like John, focusing on the power of the people who believe in us at various points in our lives. This project is my way of passing on and paying forward the unparalleled experience of having someone believe in you, even when you might not believe in yourself.

Through my work, I often come across young adults who have so much talent and ability. Over the years, I have consciously shown acts of kindness and support to this next generation of leaders, business people, artists, parents, and citizens so they will begin to believe in themselves, just like John believed in me. It's personally rewarding and gratifying to watch them spread their wings and soar!

Behind the Scenes Takeaway

As I reflect on this time in my life, I recognize the importance of seeing the significance in others before they see it in themselves. I also recognize you can't orchestrate these kinds of relationships or write up a plan outlining how and when they are going to happen. We never can know for sure when one is believing in us, or we are the ones believing in someone else. All of us have that person inside us waiting to be released. It's simply a matter of when...and who will be the catalyst for that moment.

Key Question for Personal Reflection

When was the first time you began to believe in yourself?

Walking toward Greatness

by Tristan James

Honoring Donald Hitt

I believe everything happens for a reason. I don't believe I went through the things I've been through "just because." Once you believe that everything happens because it's part of your destiny, the enemy -- whether you believe it's the world or yourself -- can only keep you down for so long.

But that's hard. When you're a kid opening the cabinets and all you see are cans of pears and peaches because that's all you have... or you see your mom pick up the food stamp check in the mail... or you see bed bugs scurrying across your mattress in the homeless shelter you're staying at... that affects you when you're young. You don't think there's a way out.

Add to the equation losing your dad when you're 15 years old and it feels like life couldn't get any bleaker.

Like most boys, my dad, Randy James, was my hero growing up. He was not only my dad. He was my friend, my advisor, my counselor. We were so close and we were just there for each other. Things didn't work out between him and my mom, but he remained a steady and important influence in my life until he passed. He'd been having chest pains for about six months before he was admitted to the ICU. He'd had tests run and they'd all come back clean. No sign of heart disease. Yet he continued to have chest pains. The medical professionals couldn't figure out what was going on with him.

When he called me the night before he went into the ICU, he said he had come home early from work that day and was still having chest pains. He wanted to tell me he was looking forward to spending Easter weekend with me.

After that, he went for a walk with his new wife, Tina. They'd been married for about a month. The call and the walk were several things in a series of firsts for my dad. Whether you believe it or not, those firsts signified something was happening. I had a sense something wasn't right.

On the morning of Good Friday, I woke up early and took a long shower. Soon afterwards, Tina called and told me Dad had gone into a coma. He was in a coma for the next two weeks.

When Dad's body started shutting down, he had to be medevacked to another hospital where they could perform therapeutic hypothermia to prevent any further damage to his organs. He had been there for about an hour or two, and everything seemed to be going fine. Then we heard someone calling over the intercom, "Medical ICU! Medical ICU! Code blue! Code blue!"

My dad's heart had stopped and he needed immediate help to get it going again. Tina and I stood at the doors of the ICU, waiting to find out what would happen. The nurse came out and informed us of the situation.

So much was happening at once. It was hard to process it all.

It felt like the world as I knew it was swallowing me whole.

Dad passed away on May 6th. Losing him sent me on a search to fill the void, the hole he left behind. Sometimes what fills that void comes in a different shape, size or person than what you thought.

But the Universe has a funny way of giving us just what we need when we need it.

That void was filled for me by Donald Hitt. He was my high school speech coach. I competed in an activity called Forensics, but I'd only competed one time when I lost Dad and had to drop out to attend to family matters.

When I returned to school the following year, Mr. Hitt wanted to talk to me. I'd only known him for a little while, but in the short time I had known him, I'd developed a sense of awe and wonder in his presence. He was a Hall of Fame coach who had won 16 state championships in Forensics and four Theater state championships with the teams he'd coached.

To be honest, I was scared to talk to him because Mr. Hitt demanded excellence. If you were going to be on his team, you'd better show up and do what he said. Because of losing Dad, I hadn't shown up and met his expectations for excellence.

I sat in his office and waited for a lecture. I fully expected him to read me the riot act about dropping out, and you'd better believe I was scared!

But he didn't lecture me or chastise me for leaving the team. Instead, what he said next nearly knocked me out of my chair.

He said, "Son, I would like you to come with us to the national tournament. I think it would be beneficial to you."

After my initial shock, I gathered my wits about me and explained how going wouldn't be possible for me. Number 1: my family didn't have money, and it would be hard for me to afford the trip; and number 2, my dad had recently passed away.

He said, "Son, I already know all about that, and I'm sorry about your dad. I know you don't have the finances for it, which is why you're going to go anyway. You just come."

He paid my way out of his own pocket.

From that point on, every time we got on the bus to compete -- and we competed most Saturdays throughout the three years I was under his guidance -- he handed me a $20 bill so I could get something to eat. He saw something in me and believed in me, even after I had to step away for a while.

His invitation to go with him and the team changed my life. He didn't want my poverty or the loss of my dad to be reasons I didn't succeed. He took those excuses away from me right from the start. I'm not sure where I'd be today if he hadn't.

Forensics is very rigorous. It requires everyone on the final stage to wear a black suit. I only had a blazer, khakis and a pair of Sperry's. If I ever was going to be anything on the national stage, I would have to wear a black suit.

When I qualified for the national tournament my sophomore year, Mr. Hitt said, "Son, let's get you a suit."

He took me to Burlington Coat Factory, and he bought me a black suit and a pair of black shoes. Those shoes became very important because I could change out the shirt and the tie, but I always wore the same shoes. They were a symbol of me **walking toward something greater.** The shoes told me, *I'm not limited or bound.* They represented Freedom!

When I put those shoes on and started to win, I started to believe in myself. I could walk away from what was going on at home. I could walk away from being a victim of my circumstances and toward being a victor, doing things other people said I couldn't.

Every time I stepped on a stage. Every time I competed. Every time I performed. As long as I put those shoes on and did what I was best at, I could walk away from all the things that were trying to pull me down and keep me in a place of poverty and pain.

I still wear those shoes today.

The timing of Mr. Hitt seeing something in me couldn't have been better. In hindsight, it almost seems divine. He didn't just give me an opportunity to grow through tangible resources. He counseled me and mentored me, giving me what I needed to work through my emotions and develop a stronger mindset.

Mr. Hitt took the talent I had and cultivated it, giving it a meaning and a purpose. That was a new experience for me. Up until then, I was walking around with a blindfold on, wondering what I was going to do. I had a doctorate degree in junk food and a master's degree in playing video games. I had no direction, no purpose, and no drive. I was the poster child for a lack of ambition.

Once I started winning tournaments, once I started seeing the effect of my speaking on audiences and judges, I started to believe my dreams could come true. I learned and accepted the idea that whatever you can conceive and believe, you can achieve.

There was no logical reason why a boy who came from poverty and was living in a homeless shelter should be beating people who looked better than he did. Logic would suggest that aesthetics alone would have determined the outcomes of those tournaments. It would suggest that as I stood next to my opponents looking shabby and poor, the judge would have automatically selected the better looking candidate.

That's not what happened, though. I showed up and competed, always giving it my best. I was able to bring characters from a script to life and touch the audience. I learned so much at those tournaments about performance and people. That led to seven state championships and a 7th place finish my senior year in high school. I received the award for Virginia Student of the Year from the National Debate and Speech Association.

Each experience allowed me to walk in different character's shoes. Each character and situation I came across helped me understand how everyone is walking toward greatness in their own way, just like I am.

As a result, I am fortunate to be attending Virginia Commonwealth University. I live with a man named Ryan Kopacsi, who is the director of the VCU Pep Band. He is the quintessential example of a perfectionist and has very high expectations. When I first moved in, he said, "You need to dress better."

It felt like a slap in the face. I was offended and wanted to say, "Do you have any idea what I've been through?" I started playing the victim tape in my head.

But the more I thought about it, the more I realized his point was not a slight. If I truly want to be one of the big players, I have to roll like a big player.

These days you won't catch me without a collared shirt on. Dressing up doesn't make me better than other people. It merely reflects the decision I've made to show up as my fullest self. I had bought into the idea that if you dressed like a rich person, then you wouldn't care about other people or forget where you've come from. But that simply isn't true.

When others care about you, they will put pressure on you to live your life accordingly. Ryan has taught me that if I want others to respect me, I need to do things a certain way and present myself a certain way. It's not about the clothes. It's about the expectations. If you're really going to be who you say you are, you need to live up to them.

When someone is hard on you, it's not because they don't like you or you are a jerk. It's because they see something more in you and they know if they're not hard on you, you will never rise up and meet your potential and receive the rewards you deserve. We all have the ability to walk toward greatness. It may take someone from the outside like Donald Hitt did for me to point us in the right direction. In the end, though, it's up to us to put one foot in front of the other as we take the stage for the rest of our lives.

People tell me all the time, "Tristan, you're an old soul."

I don't believe that. I believe I realized who I am earlier than most people do. Because of this, I'm able to attract great things into my life and stay above forces that try to pull me down. But none of my current success would have been possible if Mr. Hitt hadn't let me know he believed in me. His compassion taught me to believe in myself. His support became a golden memory that is now part of my DNA.

If you believe in something and you want something to happen, you have to do something about it. Results don't just magically appear out of thin air. If you believe in someone, their talents and gifts, they won't be cultivated unless you tell them, "Hey, you're really good at this! If you keep working at it, you're going to be really successful someday."

If people don't hear that, they will continue to wander around with no will, no focus. If Mr. Hitt hadn't pointed things out for me, I'd still be walking around with a blindfold on.

Napoleon Hill, author of the iconic book *Think and Grow Rich* and father of the modern personal development movement, talks about how some of his greatest friends were people with whom he had imaginary councils. These could be people who were dead or influencers of his time. He would sit down, close his eyes, and pretend they were in the room with him. He would meditate on the idea that Thomas Edison was sitting next to him, answering all his questions.

I've adopted this approach. Some of my best friends are dead or come to me through the books I read. It's like this with Dad. He can always be with me as long as I give presence to him and honor him. What I know now is because of him, not despite him.

Even though I no longer see Mr. Hitt every day, he continues to influence my life in this way. The lessons and principles about success he taught me are with me all the time. He taught me to look within, and that's where it all begins. I can only hope to pass on what he taught me as I continue building the lineage we are all a part of. If I can be a force that believes we have the ability to sort through our differences and have kinder conversations, I will have succeeded beyond my wildest dreams.

Behind the Scenes Takeaway

Tristan has one of the most commanding and powerful voices I have ever heard. When interviewing him, I was initially caught off guard and then mesmerized by the sound coming over Skype as he told me his story. One of my biggest takeaways is how generous he is with his time to openly talk about the way Donald Hitt took away every reason he could have used for not doing something with his life. Poverty and loss of his dad could have stopped him from realizing his full potential, but the timing of Mr. Hitt extending a hand could not have been better. For anyone working with young people, this story is a perfect example of how seeing raw talent, believing in it, and encouraging it can make a difference.

Key Question for Personal Reflection

When did someone in your life help you overcome your self-limiting beliefs?
Who was your Mr. Hitt?

The Collie Factor

by Brad Ball

Honoring Bob "Collie" Colombatto

Some people have a knack for seeing the gifts and talents in others. They say things such as, "I like the way this guy is figuring things out," and from there begin the shaping and guiding process. That was Bob "Collie" Colombatto for me when I first started my career in advertising. He was a teacher, a mentor, a friend, and a boss. Working together for 23 years, we were like a couple of songwriters, always experimenting with a new tune. We shared a vision about seeing things bigger, whether the ad was on a national account or we wanted the campaign to have a greater impact. **I called this the "Collie Factor"** because he always created messages that were much bigger than the product or service the ad campaign was about. He was hard to work for, but because we had mutual respect, our relationship was harmonious and rewarding.

Collie cofounded an independent ad agency called Davis, Johnson, Mogul & Colombatto with his childhood friend from Berkeley, California, Bob Davis. It would become Davis, Ball & Colombatto in the 1980s and is currently DavisElen Advertising. Both Bob and Collie became teachers as well as partners. Collie not only impacted my life and influenced me during my tenure there, but he continues to influence me today, all these years later.

We had a father-son relationship that, together with Bob, evolved to a partner relationship--never the boss but, rather, an equal. Our connection was more like Nala in *The Lion King* in that Collie passed the leadership mantle on to me. He gave me the confidence to believe in my crazy ideas, and he also had the confidence in handing over the reins.

I loved working at DJMC. We lived for the business. Collie was on the creative side of the agency, and Davis was on the business side. Between those two personalities, Collie was the hot Chinese mustard and Davis was the soothing ketchup you'd put on your dim sum. They had a good recipe for partnering, which is why the agency succeeded. Davis made clients feel like they were the most important account. Collie made clients feel uncomfortable, pushing them to the creative edge so they would get attention in the marketplace. They, in turn, loved him for it.

The bottom line is: he taught me to trust my instincts. When I think about all the hours Collie and I spent together throughout the years, nobody else comes close to giving me the foundation of how I think about business. To this day, no matter what I'm doing, I can still hear Collie's voice coaxing me along, saying, "Go for it! Don't make this all look the same."

I developed my passion for advertising as a kid. I was born in 1950, right on the cusp of the Baby Boomer generation. My dad grew up in a house that was built in the 1920s. When I went to my grandmother's house with my two brothers, I snuck down into the basement where she had every issue of *Life* magazine from the very first. The basement smelled musty and was dark, but it was also a secret place to go. Every new *Life* I opened made me say, "Wow! Look at this." I was most interested in the ads and how cool they looked. I laughed at the references to old cars. Many of the ads used images or words that would be considered politically incorrect today. I spent hours with those magazines and brought home copies. I still have many copies of those *Life* magazines today.

Those magazines captured my attention with respect to the power of the advertising medium, an early indicator of the creative career I was heading toward. My mother had other ideas. She told me, "You're really good at speeches and debate. Why don't you become a lawyer?" That sounded boring to me. I came from four generations of doctors, but I wasn't about to become one. I saw how thick those medical books were and how tiny the writing was. I thought about how badly I'd done in chemistry and physics. (Not a single frog I dissected came back from the dead!)

I said, "I may have the bedside manner in my DNA, but I don't want to become a doctor." I wanted to be in a field where I could balance telling jokes and having fun. The movie business was more my style, something highly creative. In my spare time in junior high and high school, my friends and I made Super 8 movies. We started a company called Lodestone Comedies and made about ten films. Our tag line - Brevity is the soul of wit – summed up our attempt at slapstick...or more like slapschtick!

I'd also done some radio shows through student government in high school. Once I was in college at USC, I did radio shows and majored in film and television. It dawned on me one day that advertising was my calling and passion, so I began searching for interview opportunities in that industry. I believed advertising was the perfect blend of creativity and business and would be a good fit for me. You had to come up with ideas, but they had to serve a business goal and deliver on that business goal. I liked that.

My first interview after graduation was with Jay Ward, the guy who created the *Rocky and Bullwinkle* series. I thought I really wanted to get in on the writing side with that company. Jay Ward was a spitting image of Captain Crunch. He was a little guy with a blond mustache and even though they didn't have any openings for me, it was still good to meet him. That's when a fraternity brother of mine, John Turner, helped get me into the mailroom at Davis, Johnson, Mogul & Colombatto.

I wasn't in the mailroom very long. Collie pegged me early and believed in me at the dawn of my career. Because of this, I soon found myself working around creatives. Eventually an opening came up on the McDonald's account. I told him I really wanted to become a copywriter, but he encouraged me to get on the McDonald's account for the experience. I could always write on the side. Like everything else he said to me, this was excellent advice.

When we would see a new business prospect or sit in meetings, I'd get ideas and share them with Collie. He'd lean in to me and say, "That is a fantastic idea, but don't tell them yet. I don't want them to think we came up with it in ten minutes. We won't be able to bill them as much!" He had an innate ability to go for the gist of any situation and ask, "What is this thing really about?"

He taught me how to think differently, but what really made working together so good for us was we could quickly arrive at a creative idea or the germ of one and then dress it up with all the strategy. Consequently, he and I became really close. One thing he did more than anything is remind me about what I was good at. He was fond of telling me I had the fastest mind in the West.

He also liked to say, "Don't doubt yourself." Sometimes you need to hear something like that from the outside, especially when you're young and still learning your craft, something more than your own inner voice helping you along the way. Hearing someone who believes in you tell you,

"Here is why this works" can go a long way. Collie was that voice for me, to the point where he was eventually confident enough to have me head up the creative department and manage all the other creatives.

The first thing you have to do when you get into a new position is understand the lay of the land. Next, you have to master two things to succeed in the creative industry: you have to have really thick skin; and you have to learn how to cherish rejection because it makes you stronger. You fight for the idea. I got to practice that a lot as I moved up the ladder.

The promotion was flattering on one hand; on the other, it made me realize I had bigger goals. Once I achieved becoming Creative Director, I next wanted my name on the door. Creativity is very subjective. If you're going to stand up in front of your client or peers and say, "This has to be red" and they argue, "No, it's gotta be blue," you can then walk them to the front of the building, point, and say, "See that name on the door? Red is better than blue." You win all subjective arguments when your name is on the door.

During my time as the Creative Director, I produced and wrote a lot of material. When business was getting tougher, Collie and Davis decided to promote me to President of the agency. Even at that point when my role shifted dramatically, Collie was right by my side, cheering me on and believing in me.

I have several favorite memories of working with Collie. One of DJMC's earliest clients was always my favorite: the Bandini Fertilizer account. Collie gave me the assignment. They were located in Vernon, California, right off the freeway. I went out there, saw the factories and all the piles of manure and said, "I got it! Bandini Mountain, man dares to go where only cows have gone before!" So I grabbed my Super 8 camera, climbed up the pile with my skis, skied down it, came back to the office and showed Collie.

He said, "This is brilliant! No one wants to think about smelly fertilizer. We're going to have a lot of fun with this!"

Collie wrote the original campaign. It was, "Bandini is the word for fertilizer." A legend named June Foray, who had a really sexy voice and was the earliest pioneer in voice animation characters with close to 300 characters to her name including Smurfs and the grandmother in Tweety Pie and most of all Natasha and Rocket J. Squirrel in *Rocky and Bullwinkle*, came on board and did the voiceover for the Bandini campaign. It ran for years and is one of my claims to fame.

Collie was passionate about everything. He loved his business and the people he worked with. I'll never forget when he pitched McDonald's for the first time back in the late '60's. He rode into the room on an elephant. There were 60 to 80 people there to hear the presentation.

He said, "I just have to say this about my commitment to you if you give us your account. I've been thinking about this. I am so committed to it; I can feel this brand in my heart."

Then he unbuttoned his shirt and revealed a Big Mac tattooed on his chest. People talked about that for years.

Finally, I'll never forget the day he returned from a business trip to New York. He called me, foaming at the mouth with excitement. He had sat next to John DeLorean on the plane and thought we were going to get the car account. I asked him why he believed that.

He said, "This guy DeLorean used to run the Pontiac division at General Motors, and he's going to make a brand new car called the DeLorean."

Turns out, he did. As a result, Collie and Davis were the first two guys in the state of California to get DeLoreans.

Unfortunately, Collie developed poor health in his later years. First he suffered a stroke, then he had back surgery, followed by a second stroke. He also had a bad heart, so by the time he was 50 and I was in my early 30s, he was less involved with the business. I became the surrogate partner to Bob Davis. Some personal issues took an even greater toll on Collie's health, but he was influential in the business well into his 70s. His brain and remarkable take on the advertising world continued to his last days.

Through my teaching at USC today, I pay forward many of the lessons Collie taught me. It's going to sound like the biggest cliché, but if you don't believe in what you're doing, who will? At the end of the day, you need to be prepared to fight your instincts to give up if you choose to go down a hard path. If you have somebody in your life who doesn't want you to give up, that's the best thing you could possibly have. Two people getting behind a creative idea is always better than one.

Collie helped me hone my persuasive skills, but he also helped me see things through that I believed in. If I could thank him today, I would point out how fortunate it was for me to connect with someone like him who understood the way I think and to inspire me with the way he thought. As hard as I worked and with the inevitable moments of fear I faced along the way, Collie was always a steady force, assuring me I'd get through the challenges. He had confidence in me and my abilities. If something didn't work, it didn't work. It wasn't the end of the world.

He believed if we were going to be successful, it didn't matter where an idea came from. It was more important to keep the end result top of mind. Second only to coming up with an idea is seeing it come to life. Collie also gave Davis confidence when he lost his partner he'd grown up with. Davis could trust Collie to keep things going in his absence. Putting my name on the door was a big deal and signified just how much Collie and Bob believed in me.

Collie proved coming up with ideas is a great way to make a living. Throughout my career working for myself, other agencies, Warner Brothers movie division, NASCAR, McDonald's Corporation, and now Sky Zone, I have often asked myself, *If Collie were here, how would he do this?* He influences me still to this day, all the time!

My career has remained interesting and personally rewarding over time, and I have no plans of slowing down anytime soon. I've been fortunate to work with some of the most creative and brilliant minds in the entertainment industry including Steven Spielberg, Jeffrey Katzenberg, and even J.K. Rowling. When I think of the clients, movies and businesses I've been in, I'm both humbled and amazed. My adventure book has some very cool chapters in it, but I'd argue the best one of all is the one titled, "The Collie Factor."

Behind the Scenes Takeaway

I have known Brad for almost 30 years. An interesting side note is as we talked, I realized I had interviewed him for a paper I wrote for a marketing class when I was in college! In many ways, Brad was still like the young man I remember all those years ago, leaning forward on the lunch table recalling the great adventure he'd had with Collie. It was so much fun watching him go down memory lane. One of my biggest takeaways from his story is how far words of encouragement and belief can go in developing confidence in raw, young talent in our workplaces. Once someone's recognized, the foundation is set for their success as they move through their careers, relationships, and lives. I love how Collie's relationship with Brad was the sweetest combination of all: a boss, a teacher, a mentor, and a friend.

Key Question for Personal Reflection

What was the most uplifting piece of advice you've ever received?

The Currency of Confidence

by Dr. Bill Dorfman

Honoring Barbara Dorfman

Sometimes in life, you have to pick and choose your mentors and what they're mentoring you for. It's very rare to find everything in one mentor, but it is possible to have one consistent force throughout your life, that one person who believes in you no matter what. This has been true for me. I've had several mentors at different points along my personal and professional journey. Each one has helped shape me, my dental career, and my business success. Each one has invested **the currency of confidence** in me in their own, special way.

I learned about marketing, business and networking, for example, from my grandfather. He worked his way up through the ranks in the liquor industry and eventually became the CEO of a company, taking it from nothing to a multibillion dollar enterprise. I learned about the importance of philanthropy and giving back from my high school biology teacher who organized trips to deliver food and gifts to needy families in Los Angeles during the holidays. I learned how to promote myself and build a multimillion dollar dental practice from the late Dr. Jeff Golub Evans, who was the past president of the American Academy of Cosmetic Dentistry. I learned patience and how to be a gentleman from my father. I learned about fundraising for a nonprofit organization through my work with the Smiles for Life and LEAP Foundations; I was instrumental in helping to start both programs. But the steadiest and most consistent influence throughout my life from its very inception has been, hands down, my mom, Barbara Dorfman.

My mom is amazing. The greatest gift she gave me was the gift of confidence. She made me believe I could do whatever I wanted, for better or for worse. Thank goodness we didn't live in a two-story house when I was growing up because I literally would have thought I could fly. And believe me, I made a lot of mistakes that could have turned out to be disastrous. But even in the wake of mistakes, I grew up never doubting myself. I never operated inside a box the way a lot of kids around me did. I honestly didn't know a box existed. Instead, I always pushed the pedal to the metal and did more than what anyone ever expected.

Ever since I can remember, Mom has been a rock holding our whole family together. She was 18 when she got married. She had three young boys by the age of 24 but discovered she was not married to the right man. My biological father was a mess. My mom had the courage to leave him and raise us on her own. Back in the 1960s, leaving your husband to go out on your own was unheard of. The support we have today for single mothers wasn't available. Furthermore, divorce was uncommon and had a negative stigma attached to it. She didn't finish college, so she had no professional skills to draw on for work. Even with three boys to support and no immediate job prospects on the horizon, she knew we'd be better off without him.

Fortunately, she remarried a man who I came to consider my only father. He was the complete opposite of my biological dad. He raised my brothers and me and was a great role model. He is intellectual, calm, mild-mannered and a real gentleman. I learned a lot from him about what it means to be a man. Watching him treat my mother with love also taught me a lot about respecting women and our family.

One day when I was walking home from school, I had an epiphany. I was in first grade, and I'd just learned how to read. In my 6-year-old mind, I had convinced myself that, since I knew how to read, what did I have to go to school for?

I couldn't wait to get home and tell my parents this incredible news! I walked in and announced, "Guess what? I don't need to go to school anymore."

They looked at me, then at each other. "What do you mean, you don't need to go to school anymore?"

I said, "Well, I know how to read now, so I'll just read everything." This kind of thinking made complete sense to me.

But they were having none of it. "Ahh, no," they said. "You still need to go to school."

I didn't understand their perspective, but there was no way I was going to convince them otherwise. It didn't turn out to be such a bad thing, after all. I'm grateful they had my best interests at heart.

Staying in school provided the academic foundation I needed for my dental career. A lot of people grow up struggling with what they want to do in life. I didn't.

Way before my reading epiphany, at the age of 2 ½, I had an accident and knocked out my front teeth. Our family dentist put me back together again. As he was taking me through multiple surgeries and procedures, I kept thinking about how cool it would be to someday do what he was doing to me. Instead of being scared by the procedures, I was intrigued by them. When all the other kids in my class wanted to be firemen, policemen and soldiers in the army, I wanted to fix teeth.

Knowing what I wanted to do made my journey through school easier. I knew which classes I needed to take in college. In fact, one of the first things I did after graduating from dental school was find the five best dentists in LA and shadow them. No one told me to do this. I did it on my own, drawing innately on the currency of confidence that my mom invested in me from day one.

I wanted to learn everything I could from the best of the best because, even then, I knew it was much easier to copy genius than reinvent mediocrity. I've been wired to think like this since I can remember.

Mom knew I wasn't like my brothers or any other kid for that matter. I grew up one of four brothers and a sister, and they are all great individuals. We are each different, unique in our own ways. In her innocence, she simply wanted the best for all of us, which is why she sometimes used me as the example of how the rest needed to be.

I remember one day in particular when I was quite young. I was in one room of the house and Mom was in another. She didn't know I was there. She was coming down hard on my three brothers for not measuring up to me.

After she was done, I confronted her.

I said, "Mom, please never do that again. You will make my brothers hate me. I am not a good example of 'normal.' I have never been 'normal,' and I will never be 'normal.' There is something really unusual about me. I don't know what it is, but it's been that way from the time I was an infant. You can't expect other kids to be like me. I am what I am and you just have to appreciate that. Don't compare them to me because, if you do, I will lose my relationship with them." I value and love the relationship I have with my siblings.

After high school, I attended UCLA. I questioned whether it was the right place for me after the first quarter ended. I came from a large high school where I knew everybody, and for people who did not know me well, at least they knew I was David's or Gary's brother. I felt very comfortable with those references because people knew my family.

Things were different at UCLA. In a sea of 30,000 students, I didn't feel welcome at all. In addition, I didn't even do well academically right away. I was in the pre-dental program, and one of my childhood friends was pre-med. He was our class valedictorian and we both received scholarships. We also both took the same courses. That first term I got a B, C, and a Pass. I was really bummed out about that. Turns out, my friend did worse.

In those days, you received your scholarship check for tuition and living expenses right before school started so you could pay all your registration fees. He didn't come from a wealthy family. The day before the second quarter started, he had apparently cashed his scholarship check and given the money to all his friends. I was thinking how weird the situation was. I wondered where he could have gotten all that money. And why was he giving it away?

Then, the night before school started, he jumped off the top of the dorm. I was in shock. It was a rude awakening for me and made me question everything.

I called my parents and told them what happened. They were shocked to hear about my friend.

After talking through the situation for a while, I said, "I don't know how I'm going to get into dental school with my grades."

I was noticeably concerned, and Mom must have sensed I was really feeling low.

She said, "Honey, you will just do something else."

I said, "You don't understand, Mom. I have always wanted to be a dentist."

"You'll be good at something else, Bill. Don't worry," she said, trying to reassure me like she always did.

But I insisted. "No, Mom. I'm going to be a dentist."

After that, it was the only "C" I ever got at UCLA and, in fact, I almost got straight A's until I graduated.

Four years later when I graduated, I was honored with an award the university bestows upon the top three seniors in the class called "The

Outstanding Senior Award." Right after the Chancellor's office called to congratulate me, I called my parents to tell them.

I said, "Mom, Dad, you won't believe this, but I just got a call from the Chancellor's office. I won the "Outstanding Senior Award" at school!"

At first, they didn't say anything.

I continued. "Mom, do you know how big this is?"

Finally, she said, "Sweetie, do you honestly think there is anybody better?"

That's how much she believed in me.

I said, "You're missing the point."

"But seriously. Who else would they give it to?" she continued, oblivious to how small the odds were of winning that award.

I said, "Mom, there are 10,000 people in the class to give it to!"

But it wasn't until we got to the ceremony in my honor with 500 people in the room when my mom looked at me and said, "Wow! This really is a big deal."

"Mom, I know!" I said, exasperated and relieved at the same time.

Mom was clueless about some things. It was actually kind of cute. Looking back, it's amazing how much she just believed in me. The currency of her confidence never ran out. It was like a secret gold mine running underneath my life that I could draw on in any situation.

I believe it's one of the main sources of my professional success today. Over the years, I've been interviewed by a lot of famous talk show hosts on TV, including Oprah. Normally when you are a guest on a show like *Ellen* or *Rosie*, a producer asks you questions for an hour or two in a pre-interview. Then the questions you answer the way they like most are the ones they will ask you for the show. They pick the best of the best and bring you out front where they ask you those same questions again in a six-minute segment.

There have been only two times when this didn't happen to me. One was on *Larry King Live*, which was truly a live show. The other time was with Oprah. Oprah doesn't do a pre-interview because Oprah wants your raw, unfiltered response.

When I was on her show, she said to me, "Dr. Bill, what do you think makes you unique? I mean, *really, really* different?"

I told her what really makes me different is when I get an idea, and I believe in that idea, I execute it! I refuse to give up and will do whatever it takes to make that idea succeed. When I founded Discus Dental with two of my closest friends, all I had was an idea, and together we worked to create the largest tooth whitening company in the world. We grew the company from zero to over $1.3 billion in cumulative sales. A large part of why I believed in myself was because my mom and dad believed in me. That unshakable faith carried me forward even when other people thought I was crazy. I have also been an independent freethinker for as long as I can remember. I don't let "no" get in the way of anything I want to do.

We can never stop learning or get complacent. We always must remain open to learning new things. We can always be better tomorrow than we are today. And perhaps most importantly, we can't wait for opportunities in life, we must create them. When a new opportunity does come along, don't just take it -- MASTER it. I have my family, and especially my mom, to thank for everything.

Behind the Scenes Takeaway

When I first met Dr. Bill, I was struck by his warmth and friendly demeanor. I could see in his smile the pride he has for his mom, a reflection of the confidence he's developed and has used to open many doors. One of the biggest takeaways from his story is we all have many mentors throughout our lives, but a mother's steady and constant love can run circles around all the mentors we encounter combined. When parents believe in their children, those kids have a stronger chance of believing in themselves, becoming wildly successful, and mastering their lives.

Key Question for Personal Reflection

Who has been the most steady and consistent force in your life?

The Measuring Stick

by Melissa Nickelson

Honoring Mrs. Rita Palm

In elementary school, I had a teacher who told me I would become Miss America one day. She based this statement on what everyone bases a statement like that on: what someone looks like. With my blond hair and blue eyes, I have the typical all-American appearance that the pageantry industry is known for using to measure a woman's worth. Those teacher's words could have forever shaped the course of my life had I not eventually met Mrs. Rita Palm and discovered achievement and success extend beyond what a woman looks like.

I met Mrs. Palm when I was in high school. This was back in the day when women like her were always called "Mrs. So and So" and never by their first name. I was dating a boy who was friends with her son Chris. My boyfriend and Chris were a year older than I was, and we would go to the Palms' house periodically. This is how I got to know her. I talked to her several times, and I imagine she was drawn to me because I was the only girl with three boys hanging out at her house. I also happened to be the most consistent girlfriend of all those guys. The Palms lived in a beautiful home, and she and her husband were very politically connected. She and her husband owned several businesses, did prison ministry, and together they shared deeply committed Christian values. They were generous with both their time and money and gave back to the community.

One day I mentioned to Chris I was looking for a job.

He said, "You know, my mom is looking for someone."

I was only 15 at the time and wasn't even driving yet, but I called her anyway and learned she was looking for an assistant. She was a Shaklee Distributor, selling their cleaning and beauty products. She hired me and I started helping her run the business, answering the phone, filling orders, placing orders, getting things ready for the UPS guy to pick up, mailing letters, and restocking the shelves – whatever she needed.

In addition to being a successful businesswoman, Mrs. Palm was appointed to several boards and organizations. I can't tell you how many political figures I talked to on the phone because of her role and connections. It wasn't long after I started working for her when I found myself typing a correspondence on her behalf to President George H. W. Bush. This was back in the day of typewriters and carbon paper, so if you messed up, you had to start all over again or use a ton of white out.

Composing her correspondence, I had to make sure it looked good. I typed faster than she did, so when she needed a letter she'd say, "Melissa, you ready?"

She would pace around the room, thinking about what she wanted to say, and I'd wait and then start typing. This experience made me realize that what you send out in correspondence and how you talk to people on the phone is a direct reflection of you. Whatever goes out with your name on it, even if someone else from your office sends it, needs to be a reflection of you. That is a big thing for me now working in the legal field. Anyone I refer people to is a reflection of me, and I take that very seriously.

The Palms were from a world that was altogether different from the one I knew. For one, Mrs. Palm got a new car frequently because she was one of Shaklee's top distributors. She hosted luncheons at her house to honor important people like Barbara Bush. My parents divorced when I was very young. Growing up, I lived with my mom and we didn't have much money. My mom did the best she could, but she grew up on a farm and she wasn't exposed to the social etiquette of a metropolitan environment. Because of this, Mrs. Palm saw herself as not just a mentor to me, but as a second mom, too. She wanted me to learn the lessons my mom couldn't teach me because my mom hadn't experienced them.

One day at work, I was sitting on the floor wrapping up vitamins and packing them in boxes to ship to her customers. I was really upset because my boyfriend and I had been fighting.

She could sense something was different and said, "You want to tell me what's wrong?"

I said, "Well, my boyfriend and I had a big fight."

"Do you want to talk about it?" she asked.

Now this was my boss! I probably would not have told my mom about my boyfriend troubles. But I heard myself opening up to her and sharing what was going on. She listened, never judging.

Finally, she said, "Do you think you could change that? What would you want to do differently about this situation?"

These questions really made me stop and think. No one had ever presented me with the idea that maybe I had options. I didn't have to settle for what was going on; I had the ability to make a choice about my life.

That included college. Mrs. Palm came from a very well-to-do family and went to college in the 1950s, something not every young woman had the opportunity to do. My mom never went to college, so when the time came for me to start considering what I'd do after high school, Mrs. Palm is the one who pushed me in that direction.

She would say, "Melissa, how are your grades? And what about college?"

When I told her I didn't know, she took charge and made things happen. She would bring college brochures to me and lay them on the table, saying, "Okay, so which one do you like?" Then she would talk to me about them.

The first time I went to look at a college and stay overnight, she took me. She had a business trip in Austin, and I liked Southwestern University. So she called them, set up the overnight visitation, dropped me off, and said, "I'll be back tomorrow to pick you up."

Along with helping me with big life decisions like finding a college, she would also take time to explain things to me about how the world really works. One day we were in her home office. She was sitting at a side table painting her fingernails because she was getting ready for a giant luncheon and she didn't have time to go get them done. I was sitting at the desk because I'd just typed a letter for her.

She said, "Melissa, I want you to listen to this." She continued painting her nails. "Melissa, it doesn't matter how much money is in our bank account. I always feel like I'm well-to-do because I know who God is and I know I'm loved."

Deep down, I sensed it would probably take me a long time to really understand all the aspects of what she was saying. I was still caught up in my own life struggles and couldn't fully comprehend that someone like Mrs. Palm, with all her success and material comforts, could possibly know what it feels like to struggle. But like the rest of us, she knew her fair share of hard times, too. She was grateful every day for the two children she and Mr. Palm had adopted and raised as their own.

When times have been hard in my life over the years, I've recalled those words and reminded myself, it doesn't matter how much money I have because at the end of the day, people like you for who you are, not for the number in your bank account. God loves you. You could die with $2 billion to your name, but if no one likes you, what's the point?

Looking back, it was probably the most profound thing she ever said to me.

When I was a senior in high school, I was in a program where I went to school half a day and worked half a day for Mrs. Palm. Through her affiliation with the Junior League, Mrs. Palm knew the teacher who was in charge of the work program. I'd finish school for the day by noon, then go straight to Mrs. Palm's to have lunch with her. I loved soup and she would sit down with me and have soup and we would talk. She was always interested in my life and kept tabs on me and my performance in school.

She would often say, "I know there are things you need to do" because her daughter was doing those same things. "I know you have that big party tonight, so I know you need to leave work by a certain time to get ready for that…"

She was very conscientious and always had my best interests at heart. One day she said, "With the work program you're in, I know there's a club and I want you to participate in it."

Well, wouldn't you know I went on to become president of that club: DECA of Fort Worth. I never would have done it if she hadn't pushed me to do it. I learned a lot through that club. DECA is a not-for-profit student organization dedicated to preparing emerging leaders in high school and college to work in marketing, finance, hospitality and management. I had the opportunity to interview prominent members of the communities around Texas. Mrs. Palm knew the value of knowing people and wanted me to better myself. In today's terms, she really "networked me," shopping me around to her circle of influence all over Texas, allowing me to learn from that experience. When I graduated from high school, several of her customers and clients sent me graduation cards and presents because they'd gotten to know me so well from working with her for two years.

Through that same work program, Mrs. Palm learned about a scholarship from one of the teachers. The teacher told her, "I want Melissa to apply for it."

There was a mountain of paperwork and a zillion things for me to do to submit my application, but when I got to work that day she said we were going to sit down and fill it all out. She walked me through the entire process, including scheduling everything for me.

When I pointed out I'd already clocked in for the day, she didn't care.

"We could do this later," I said, but she waved me off.

"We don't have time to do this later. We're going to do this right now."

More than 100 kids applied for that scholarship and wouldn't you know, I won it. The teacher found out and called me at work, and I was so excited. So was Mrs. Palm. In fact, the teacher who was supposed to come with me to the lunch where the committee was going to present the award to me couldn't go, so Mrs. Palm went with me instead. She was so proud.

I'm not sure I could have applied for that scholarship without her help. I wasn't getting that kind of guidance at home. She knew that was what I needed. I remember thinking, *Thank goodness she knows how to do this because I would have been so lost without her help!*

Even if my efforts didn't produce a positive outcome, she showed me you could find a way to move past hearing "no" and keep going. She had a never-give-up attitude, and I've never forgotten that.

When I turned 18, she sat me down and said, "Okay, go register to vote. Here's why."

And she walked me through the importance of why you need to have a voice and why you need to vote. She didn't sway me on any party. She said, "You need to know about the person you're voting for. It is your duty to know about these things."

She also taught me the importance of dressing professionally. I had three classes my senior year, and I dressed up in slacks or a dress every day because I never knew when clients were going to show up or if I'd have to go deliver things to customers. Mrs. Palm taught me, "Melissa, you dress up, no matter what, because you never know who you're going to run into. People sometimes judge you by how you look. It may not be right but, regardless, you need to make sure you fit that part."

I still practice that approach today. Sometimes when I'm at the office in casual clothes and clients show up, I apologize. "I'm sorry," I say. "I wasn't expecting clients today." I'm never grubby, in shorts or a tee shirt, but if I'm not dressed, I feel the memory of Mrs. Palm. Even though there's more than our appearance to who we are, some people never get past that. And if you want to be successful, then you better dress that part.

The end of my senior year was approaching, and I was still working for Mrs. Palm. I was getting ready to graduate and head off to TCU. One day, we were sitting at her kitchen table. It was after lunch, and we'd had our soup.

She looked at me and said, "Melissa, I think it's time for you to expand and find a new job."

It was a beautiful day outside. Sunlight was streaming through the enormous kitchen windows, yet I felt a knot growing in the pit of my stomach as if I'd just been told of a severe tornado headed my way. I was crushed.

I said. "But I don't want a new job. Did I do something wrong?"

Mrs. Palm's tone was gentle. "No, you didn't do anything wrong. I just think it's time for you to expand. You need to see the bigger picture."

I was frozen with fear. Was she going to fire me? It was hard to understand what was happening.

Interestingly enough, a woman she knew worked for a law firm, and come to find out, the firm was looking for a runner; did she know anyone who might be a good fit?

The next thing I knew, I was interviewing for the job and eventually got it. I went back to Mrs. Palm to tell her the news.

"Good for you!" she said.

I worked as a runner for the next six months until the demands of the job began to interfere with my school schedule. Mrs. Palm said, "No problem. You can come back and work for me until you get your next job. You won't be here for very long."

She was right. It was only two months before I got my next job.

Things went like that for a while. I'd work for her for a few months and then find another job. My mom thought she was great because she taught me so many things.

And through all these changes I was experiencing out in the real world, Mrs. Palm continued to make me feel like a part of the family. When she and Mr. Palm went to visit their son at Ole Miss, they invited me to go with them for the weekend. When he graduated from military school in San Diego a few years later, Mrs. Palm flew me and his sister out there and paid for the entire trip. This was another way she helped me expand my life. When she came back from a vacation to Europe, she brought me a Louis Vuitton wallet from Italy. I was beyond thrilled because I didn't have anything like that. She also gave me wonderful Christmas gifts and she always remembered my birthday. She was thoughtful to a fault, and I've never forgotten how great she made me feel.

After high school, I attended TCU, but balancing college life with working life soon became a struggle. When my grades started to drop and I realized I was failing out of school, I was deeply ashamed to tell Mrs. Palm, mostly because I was upset with myself. I'll never forget the look on her face when I finally mustered up the courage to tell her.

She closed her eyes and hung her head. All she said was, "Oh, Melissa."

I knew I was in trouble. My stomach sunk and I remember how much worse it was telling her than it was telling my mother. I'd let her down. I knew she was disappointed because she believed I could do it, and yet I hadn't believed in myself. I think the hardest pill for her to swallow was that I had defeated myself.

But you know what? Almost as quickly as she'd processed my news, she was thinking about the future. "Okay," she said. "What's next? When are you getting registered for junior college? As long as you're going to college, it doesn't matter where you go because you'll learn something. Never feel ashamed about coming to me and telling me this."

It was just amazing. She was the one who kept saying, "Keep going, Melissa. Just keep going. I don't care how hard it is. Whatever you do, don't ever stop. Don't ever give up. Get out there and go."

And I think that was it. That's what tipped me over. To this day, I use the lessons she taught me as a **measuring stick** for how I'm doing in whatever I'm doing. Whenever I'm about to start a new venture, I still ask myself, "Would Mrs. Palm be proud of what I'm about to go do?" She set the bar high and even when I didn't live up to everything, which is human, of course -- all of us make mistakes -- she made me realize it was okay to mess up because I always had a choice to keep going and do things better the next time.

I realize now that, from day one, she was pushing me out of the nest and telling me to spread my wings and fly. I could trust myself because she trusted me. She was somewhere between a mother and a mentor -- knowing when not to push and when it was okay to challenge me to go beyond what I believed I could. Now, whenever I accomplish big things, I always think about her and have the desire to tell her about my success. She's the one who really believed in me enough to make me do the things I do and, ultimately, enjoy the rewards I get from dressing the part, never giving up and working hard, no matter what.

Behind the Scenes Takeaway

When I was interviewing Melissa, I witnessed her have an epiphany about the connection between her life today and Mrs. Rita Palm. She stopped mid-sentence and exclaimed she had become a version of the woman who believed in her. As this truth dawned on her, her face lit up, her eyes widened, and she made a swooping motion through the air with her index finger as if to say, "That's it!" One of the biggest takeaways from her story is there is always a way around a disappointment, difficulty or obstacle. Love and faith are key ingredients in measuring life's success. The secret is to choose happy and just keep going.

Key Question for Personal Reflection

What is your measuring stick for success?

A Package Combo

by Mark Lack

Honoring Craig and Sandy Lack

When I was in school, I was a teenage punk, the class clown, the guy in class who was getting B's, C's, and sometimes D's. Occasionally I'd get an A, and overall I had a 3.0 average, which isn't that bad. But the truth was, most teachers saw me and said, "Oh yeah, that's one of the trouble kids. He's not going to do anything with his life." Indeed, I wasn't exactly a role model.

That prediction about my life going nowhere could have easily come true had it not been for my parents, Craig and Sandy Lack. They are hands-down the two people who have consistently influenced and impacted my life and allowed me to become the leader I am today despite the rocky road I walked for a while.

For sure, I didn't always make my parents' job of raising me easy. Growing up, I liked sports, and so they put me in every sport you could imagine, only for me to quit not long after getting started. I would say, "I want to play soccer," and my parents would say, "Great, here's soccer." Then I would quit. Next I would say, "I want to play basketball," and they'd get me a basketball. Then I'd quit that and the cycle continued. One day they finally said, "We've got to get him to find one thing he's super passionate about because we know he'll eventually stay with something." Weirdly enough, the one thing I ultimately gravitated toward was paintball. I took to it immediately, stuck with it, and as strange as it may sound, paintball was the thing that changed my life.

Now before I tell you about my paintball journey, I need to tell you more about my parents. My father Craig is a successful entrepreneur, but when I was growing up, it wasn't always that way. It took him decades to build a thriving business. My mother, Sandy, was a phenomenal support to my dad, and together they modeled for me what a great marriage can look like and how to raise a family from a place of love and abundance. They truly were **a package combo.**

Watching my dad work for himself painted a reality for me early on that I don't have to get a job and depend on someone else for my livelihood. Instead, I can create my own abundance, my own security, and my own lifestyle. He showed me that in order to do that, however, I have to consistently invest in growing myself -- through education and doing the hard work of becoming who I need to become to create and live the life I want.

Of course, I didn't want to hear what my parents were saying when I was younger. Quite frankly, I tuned them out even though I loved them and they were giving me great advice. Like I mentioned, over the years I had my fair share of ups and downs, goofing around and testing the boundaries the way a lot of teenagers do. I thought I knew what was best for me.

I've come to learn as I've matured that it's one thing for your parents to give you good advice, but it's a whole other thing for you to grow up seeing them live by the advice they give. It's tough to listen to somebody who says, "You can do anything" if they've never done anything. It's tough to listen to health experts if they say, "This is how you're going to get in great shape," but they're not in great shape themselves. It's tough to listen to business advice from somebody who's never grown a business or financial advice for how to make money or how to invest your money from somebody who's doesn't have very much money.

My parents weren't like that. They truly walked their talk. I was an extroverted teen who definitely talked more than I listened. My dad was dedicated to lifelong learning and was fond of saying, "When you're talking, you're not learning. We always want to be learning. So make sure you're at least aware that when you're talking, you're not learning. And if you want to be learning, then you should be listening. When you're with other people, listen to them twice as much as you talk to them. Sometimes the best way to do that is to ask great questions."

These days when I'm with successful people, I follow my dad's advice. I don't make the conversation about me, but instead, I make it about them. I ask questions so I can really listen to them and their story. 'Listen twice as much as you talk' has been golden advice, for sure.

One of the other things my parents were always telling me was: "You're the sum of the five people you surround yourself with most. Be wary of the individuals you let into your life because those five people will ultimately influence who you become. If you're hanging out with the wrong people, then you're going to end up wondering things like, *Why don't I have the success that I want?"*

They taught me that if you're hanging out with five people who are stuck in limiting patterns and limiting beliefs, it shouldn't come as any surprise if you're that way, too. Very rarely is there one successful person -- and for the sake of argument, let's define success as having money and freedom -- who is hanging out with four or five other people that are lacking abundance, have a negative attitude, and are physically out of shape. It's incongruent.

Unfortunately, it's all too common today for people to be hanging out with the wrong individuals. I see it all the time in the young people I work with when they first come to me. They're keeping themselves stuck in a limiting pattern and eliminating relational capital. They wonder why nothing changes. They try to change their behavior, but they're not changing their environment. One of the biggest influences within that environment is the people who populate it. A great way of thinking about this concept is like this: if you want to get in shape, but you keep eating unhealthy foods and don't go to the gym, you won't get the new results you say you want in your life. The same principle applies to personal growth. If you want to create new results in your life, but you're still hanging out with the same five people, nothing is going to change until you surround yourself with the kind of people who will support your new growth and goals.

I'm so grateful to my parents for doing a really good job of reinforcing this concept for me and my older brother. They made sure he and I were exposed to people and opportunities that matched who we are at our core and were best for us. My brother is introverted and I'm extroverted and that's how it's always been. As we've developed into the men we are today, we've both utilized our respective strengths– his introversion and my extroversion have helped us achieve different levels of success in different areas of our lives. He's into computers and technology; I'm into leadership development, coaching, and mentoring young adults. It comes back down to my parents figuring out and identifying what our strengths and weaknesses are and what opportunities, people and experiences they could expose us to that would ultimately let us develop and grow into who we have become.

Which brings me back to my paintball story. I was fourteen and I vividly remember being in the kitchen at the house my parents live in now, begging them to get me my first paintball gun, showing them images on the computer of what I wanted to do.

"Look at this," I said, pointing excitedly at the screen. "I want to be just like these guys!"

They weren't convinced. "Mark, you've quit everything you've done so far," they said. "This isn't just a basketball and a jersey; this is an expensive hobby that you've got to spend hundreds of bucks on every weekend you go out, maybe even a couple hundred bucks or a thousand bucks on your gear. You have to be really serious about this!"

I had to argue for my case and convince them I was serious this time. I finally persuaded them, and they agreed to let me pursue paintball. I took to the sport immediately, ultimately becoming one of the best professional athletes in the world. From age fourteen to seventeen, I competed professionally and was on the best team in the world. During those years, I traveled more than a quarter million miles around the globe to places like Germany, Belgium, England, France and Amsterdam. My companions were people who were five, ten, even fifteen years older than I was, and hanging around guys in their late twenties and early thirties definitely shaped who I became at a young age. I even won the largest prize in the world at age seventeen -- $160,000 in cash in one day – turning me into a six-figure earner before graduating from high school.

That unique professional paintball experience influenced my growth in so many ways. It also gave me the belief that I can accomplish anything I want when I put my mind to it. I've done the same thing I did to succeed in paintball to succeed in business -- I channeled the mindset of becoming a professional paintball player and translated it to the process of achieving greatness and mastery in the business world. Being professional in anything is based on similar principles. Understanding and applying that thought process has allowed me to reach the top 1% in my current industry in just a few short years, all before the age of twenty-five.

The big takeaway from my story is not that you have to be in the top 1% or be professional at something to be successful, but rather, there are defining moments in your life that shape who you become. Getting to a place in your life where you look back and you realize, "Wow, all of the things my parents have been telling me were not only true because now I've experienced them...But also, they've been walking what they've been talking for as long as I can remember." How rare and incredible is that!

Some of the best mentors are the ones who don't just give great advice but also live by it. My dad has always been a role model who spoke from experience. I now recognize and appreciate all the little things he's done over the years to really create the abundance, financial freedom and security he's given me and our family. He's always walked his talk, modeling the lessons he's taught me.

I work hard to be a direct reflection of him and my mom to the best of my ability. As my mom likes to say, "Do unto others as you would want done unto you." With any of the things I teach in my programs, whether it's with other business owners or whether it's with young adults (which is where my passion lies), I work hard on impacting, educating, empowering and inspiring people to go out and make their life both personally and professionally a masterpiece, however that looks for them. Then I educate them with the tools and the mindset and possibly even the resources they'll need to create abundance in their lives, both personally and professionally, just like my parents did for me.

When I'm working with young people over an extended period of time, it's amazing to see how fast they can learn. Through my leadership work today, I have the honor of witnessing young people walk down an amazing path. Sometimes it makes me stop and think because I remember how much more growing I still had ahead of me when I was seventeen or when I was twenty-one. Now I look at myself and see I've developed and grown so much. I can only imagine what it must be like to be a parent and see your kids grow up and be seventeen and twenty-one and imagine where they'll be one day.

I gave my parents a thank you card a few months ago, and I actually have another one for them in my room right now. I'm a big advocate of thanking somebody when they are not expecting it. Most people will thank somebody when they did something for them. I like to thank people for random occasions, sending them a thank you letter just for being who they are, for being in my life. Sometimes I will reference a point in the past where I can say, "Thank you for being a great friend or mom or dad or business partner" or whatever -- it doesn't have to be a thank you card, but sometimes a handwritten object you can hold is nice. Sometimes it can just be an email or a text message, but I always recommend this to people I work with, at least to consider it – sending a random thank you letter, especially to people like your parents who are most important, makes a huge impact.

In fact, I have stacks of thank you cards in my house. That's one way to make sure I send them. I'll buy a bunch of different styles, including silly ones, fun ones, too, so I have them for all different occasions. That way, I always have one on hand for when the moment strikes. I recommend keeping the cards next to a stack of envelopes and a stack of stamps so you can just send one out in the mail immediately. My parents love getting these, telling me how proud of me they are and how happy it makes them to see what I've been able to accomplish.

I'm committed to making sure my parents are forever rewarded and know that I'm grateful and thankful for everything they've given me. The two of them combined have given me an amazing model of how to create abundance and opportunities to give to the people I serve in my work and to my own kids someday. I can trace all the success I now enjoy in my life, and my ability to positively impact people through my work, to how my parents modeled making decisions, thinking about the world, and choosing who to surround themselves with. In the end, I would say success ripples back to having two amazing parents, and I couldn't be more grateful to have the ones I have.

Behind the Scenes Takeaway

This story is a perfect example of the significant role and responsibility of parenting. When interviewing Mark, I noticed how much respect he has for his parents and the way they met him and his brother not only where they were at different stages of their lives, but also where they were as individuals. One of my biggest takeaways from his story is the power of not giving up on someone even when the situation feels up in the air with no obvious solution in sight. This clearly requires patience and a spirit of perseverance, but it's worth it. Mark is now the founder of his own company, a TV host, and an author. Allowing people the freedom to explore their options the way Mark's parents did with him can have positive, long-term effects.

Key Question for Personal Reflection

If you could create your own "Sum of 5" with anyone living or dead, who would they be and why?

A Soft Landing

by Debbie Johnston

Honoring Richard Johnston and Buddy Allen

The world can be a hard place sometimes, especially for people whose circumstances marginalize them. I've focused my life's work on elevating two specific groups of people who deserve more than their situations often allow: patients recovering from illness or those needing help through their golden years, and children without a family. My first career as a nurse in the operating room opened my eyes to the many woes people experience post-op. Hospitals these days are like slides: patients go in and slide out as quickly as possible, often resulting in grim repercussions. Witnessing this process led me to my second career as the founder of Care Advantage, a company that provides post-op patients **a soft landing** after going down the slide. We offer our clients a range of services including wound care, assistance with ambulation, and effective ways to recover from illness with a licensed therapist in the privacy of a patient's home. Finally, my most recent project -- creating a non-profit organization called Connecting Hearts -- helps match adoptable children with the best family for them. As an adopted child myself, I have a tender spot in my heart for kids and the parents who want to adopt them.

None of my professional accomplishments would have been possible had I not had people believing in me along the way. No matter what stage of life you find yourself in, you need a mentor or a coach, someone to help you get from point A to point B. The secret to achieving your goals as you follow your dreams is having a support system around you. That support can come in the form of family or friends; either kind will make your journey easier and more enjoyable.

I've been blessed to have had support from both kinds of people in my life: my first mentor was my father, Richard Johnston, followed years later by Buddy Allen, a man who started out as my lawyer and quickly became my business mentor and ultimately, my friend. Both men saw something in me when I didn't see something in myself. Had it not been for their respective support and belief in me, I may never have entered nursing, founded Care Advantage, or launched Connecting Hearts. Even though I was an overachiever when I was young, it's very likely my life would have turned out much differently had my dad and Buddy not been my champions.

Growing up, I worked and lived to prove to others that I was worthy. Kids teased me about being adopted because it was different. As a result, I developed the mindset of: *I'm going to just do better and better and better to be as good as the other kids.* And I was.

I worked really hard and was rewarded for my hard work. That work ethic has served me well, laying the foundation for my nursing career and then my venture into entrepreneurship.

I've noticed this same characteristic in the adopted kids I've worked with through Connecting Hearts. A good percentage of them are overachievers, too. Of the ones who go on to succeed, they succeed extremely well. Steve Jobs was adopted, for example. He is one of history's most famous overachievers. In hindsight, I see how being an overachiever isn't so bad, after all. It's allowed me to go after my dreams and create a terrific life for myself and the people I love.

In many ways, what I do with Connecting Hearts is what my parents did for me when they adopted me: they gave me a soft landing in life. I was adopted at age three into what would become a large "Italian" family who, to this day, loves to hate each other in the best possible way. I ended up having five siblings, four sisters and a brother. Family is everything. Wherever my career takes me, wherever my life takes me, family will always be my one constant. They have been there through thick and thin, and I know that I will always be able to count on them. This is one of the big reasons behind why I founded Connecting Hearts in 2015. I wanted to create a way to give more children the chance to become part of a family, something I was fortunate to experience myself.

My parents were amazing and always put their children first. My dad was an electrician, and my mother, Eunice, was a secretary. They worked overtime and did anything and everything they could to take us on camping trips, put us through charm school and give us as much as they could. We didn't have much money, but we had a lot of love. Love was really the cornerstone of the house I grew up in. It was the tiniest house you could possibly imagine for eight people. We had one bathroom. (Can you imagine all us girls trying to get ready at the same time?) Looking back, I wonder how on earth my parents raised six kids with what seems like so little. But they did. I'm flabbergasted, but they did. To this day, my dad says he's a rich man because he had six kids around. That was his model of wealth -- his kids.

I thought my mother was a beautiful woman, and she was. When I was a girl, I walked around thinking, *I'm going to be a secretary and look just like her.* However, my journey into nursing launched when my dad gave me a nurse's kit. I was three years old and I thought that kit was so exciting. It came with a little stethoscope and I used it to listen to everyone. I also liked to put on the little hat that came in the kit. I thought I was really cute!

Over the years, I constantly heard him say to me, "Be a nurse, be a nurse, be a nurse." I listened to him intently, and took his words to heart. In fact, I can't remember a time when my dad *wasn't* telling me that if I became a nurse, I would always be safe with a job and be able to take care of myself. Turns out, he was right. My nursing career has been very good to me, setting the stage for building Care Advantage and Connecting Hearts. He may have had only a tenth grade education, but he knew a lot about life.

He didn't just influence me in nursing, though, but in business, as well. He had a lot of dreams, including having his own campground and owning his own company. If he'd been willing to encroach on family time and finances, he could have worked to make those dreams come true. But family came first, and so his dreams stayed on the shelf. His "wish I coulda shoulda wouldas" inspired me to make things happen and go for what I wanted in life.

Buddy Allen also inspired me to make things happen for myself, but in a different way than my dad. I first met Buddy when I hired him for his legal services. I was still a practicing nurse when I got into the home health industry. I'd been working in the operating room and was seeing patients being discharged quicker and sicker, which prompted my curiosity about what was happening to them once they were sent home. That curiosity led me into my career of home health care and founding Care Advantage. It was a great time to enter the industry because hardly anyone was in it.

Once word got out about what I was doing, several hospitals wanted me to start a program for them. Buddy was with me when I was negotiating what would have been my biggest deal. I'll never forget the day. The hospital offered me an impressive salary, and for a moment, I thought I was queen for a day and had hit the lottery. But Buddy didn't like the deal they gave me one bit and nixed it right in front of me.

I couldn't believe what was happening. I remember looking at him with daggers coming out of my eyes, thinking the whole time, "I'm going to get you when we get outside!" I thought it was a great deal!

After we left the hospital, he looked at me and said, "Debbie, it's time for you to do your own thing, and I'm going to be your money partner. I understand it scares you, which is all the more reason you need to go out on your own."

I realized then that he saw more in me than I saw in myself. I didn't think I could start a business, but he thought I could. Talk about somebody influencing your life!

So he mentored me, and I earned an informal MBA under his mentorship. He was very honest, full of integrity, and brilliant beyond belief. I didn't always like what he told me I had to do, but I'm so grateful he pushed me. He was very particular about doing things right. For example, he made me write a five-year business plan, something almost unheard of today because things change so quickly. I remember thinking to myself, *I don't know why he's making me do this*, and being mad at him for it. When I finished putting my plan together, I realized that I knew everything about what running my business required, including how much money I needed to bring in to cover my costs. He pushed me past my comfort zone not for him, but for me. He wanted me to grow.

Of all the money partners he had, I was the only female. When I came up with the pink heart to use as a logo for my company, he said, "I don't know about the pink heart, Debbie."

I said, "Trust me. It's going to be fine."

And it was.

Like my father, Buddy was a significant force in my life. He taught and inspired me to become the businesswoman I am today. I never could have started Connecting Hearts nearly 30 years after starting Care Advantage, for example, had it not been for Buddy and his influence. He was the smartest businessman I've ever known, inspired by Vince Lombardi's words, *"It's not whether you get knocked down, it's whether you get back up."* On those days when I felt like life had knocked me down, Buddy was right there believing I could get back up. I can't think of enough good things to say about him.

I believe when we get to the top of the elevator of life, it's our job to go back down and get the next person. I've been at both the bottom and the top of that elevator, being brought up and then going down to bring others up. My dad and Buddy made getting to the top possible and always provided a soft landing when times were tough. Now it's my turn to be at the top of the elevator for them. My dad is 85 years old and has some health issues. Seeing him at less than 100 percent is very challenging and emotional for me.

Despite the dementia, though, he's still witty and funny. He looks like Santa Claus, and everyone loves him. I call him "Pappy." In fact, I made him a Facebook giant. Whenever I put his picture up on my newsfeed and say a little something about him, the post will have hundreds of likes almost instantly. He often gets more likes than I do!

I make a point of telling him every time I see him, "You've been the most fantastic father. You are the most fantastic father, and I love you so much." If something happens to him, I want that sentiment to be my last words to him. He smiles every time I say those words, and his smile warms my heart.

Seven years ago, Buddy developed cancer. Life has not been the same since he got sick. He is my business soulmate. With him active in my life I always felt safe, like nothing could go wrong. I've missed him so much. He's still battling the disease.

When I first went into the home health business, I had no idea what I was stepping into. I never dreamed in a million years I would own, manage, and grow businesses like CareAdvantage and Connecting Hearts. The number of challenges and hurdles to overcome were many, and Buddy was instrumental in helping me survive running a business, along with managing the responsibilities of being Virginia's adoption champion.

Today, Connecting Hearts works tirelessly to find parents for the more than 900 adoptable kids in Virginia. Matching children with adoptive parents is in my soul. I want every adoptable kid to find a home because having a family is a basic human right. I consider myself lucky for being adopted into the wonderful family I've known practically my entire life. So far, we've been successful in facilitating some good matches, and that means a lot to me. Part of my mission is to give these kids just a sliver of what I had as an adopted child, that soft landing that can make all the difference.

I think the best thing to come out of working with Buddy and the many others who are behind Connecting Hearts is that Virginia is going to be the first state to use Family Match, a match process for kids and parents looking to adopt, similar to eHarmony. We are extremely proud of this, and we feel like it's our best contribution to society so far.

If Family Match goes well, and we think that it will, then other states will use our system. Eventually, we want to see it used on a national level. Statistically, we know it will help reduce the time typically invested in the adoption process. Social workers often say, "Well, it's going to take six months…" This upsets me because six months is a long time in a kid's life. We're very hopeful that our system expedites the adoption process from start to finish, reducing the wait time and making dreams come true for kids and parents faster than ever.

In my business, I deal with a lot of "wished I would-have could-have should-haves." Making the time to tell someone how important they are to us is a gift. We don't do it enough, which is why I've made sure to let both my dad and Buddy know how much they've meant to me all these years. I've sent them cards, spent time with them, and told them directly how much they matter to me. I do my best to love and honor them every day.

My sincerest wish is for everyone to have a father and a mentor like my dad. There will never be anyone as great as he was to me, but I've found some awesome business mentors along the way, including Buddy Allen. One of my greatest personal accomplishments is loving people and being loved. Having those two remarkable men in my life is more than anyone could ever hope for, and I cherish each day I get to be with them. They each made me who I am in their own special ways, and I will always carry in my heart their memories and the lessons they taught me.

Behind the Scenes Takeaway

Debbie's life work and commitment to elevating others' lives is beyond amazing. Through her own business, Care Advantage, and her non-profit organization, Connecting Hearts, she has initiated the ripple effect so beautifully for so many deserving people. And it all started for her when her parents, Eunice and Richard Johnston, dropped the proverbial pebble into the pond of her life when they adopted her. The same can be said of Buddy when he believed in her to bravely branch out to start her own business. I admire Debbie's inclusive management style and see the direct correlation between the impact those who believed in her had on her life and the effect she has on the lives of others. She said that one of her biggest accomplishments is loving others and being loved, proving that sometimes all it takes to make small waves in our lives is simply having the love and support of others.

Key Question for Personal Reflection

Think of a time in your life when you took the elevator down to life's "lobby" to get someone and bring them to the top.

Nothing but the Best

by Robert Hayman

Honoring Fred J. Hayman and Emil Sziraki

We all experience different seasons of our lives, and occasionally, we will have an immediate connection to a specific person where a special chemistry exists that's second to none. This person could be someone from our family, a friend, or our significant other. I experienced that kind of chemistry with my maternal grandfather, Emil Sziraki, one of the two men who played a significant role in shaping me as I grew up. The other man who influenced my life was my father, Fred J. Hayman, also known as "the father of Rodeo Drive." As men and as influencers, my grandfather and my father could not have been more different, but they each shaped my life and helped me become the man I am today.

My grandfather was a bricklayer by trade; my father founded and ran one of the most iconic fashion brands of its time in the world, Giorgio Beverly Hills. My grandfather lived in a two-story, log cabin on 72 acres of farmland in a rural community outside of Mansfield, Ohio; my father lived in a townhome in one of the most expensive zip codes on the planet. My grandfather taught me how to hunt, farm, and fish; my father taught me the difference between a champagne flute and a water glass. My grandfather showed me by example how to be patient; my father exposed me to the importance of doing the right thing and being charitable. While it's true I grew up with the luxury Rodeo Drive symbolizes, I was also greatly influenced by a simpler way of life led on a farm. These lifestyle differences created a special opportunity for me to develop into someone with solid values, a strong work ethic and an appreciation for the broad spectrum of human experience.

Originally from Switzerland, my dad came to America during World War II to start a new life. The hotel business was his first venture until he found his way into the fashion industry, where he would remain for the rest of his career. I spent the first few years of my life in the Beverly Hilton Hotel where my father was the manager. He handled everything: the food, room service, the many hotel restaurants, catering, banquets and more. He rubbed elbows with very powerful people, including John F. Kennedy, who was there for the 1960 democratic national convention. Since 1961, the hotel has hosted the Golden Globe Awards every year, featuring A-list celebrities, directors, and Hollywood insiders. With help from my father, the Beverly Hilton became *the* venue in Los Angeles for practically every major event.

He had an amazing life, one most people only dream of. Not only was he stylish, but he was also honest and had a strong work ethic. Like my grandfather, he had that credo of being **nothing but the best**, doing whatever it took in an ethical way to succeed. It complemented and reinforced the lessons my grandfather was teaching me, and I paid attention.

He started Giorgio Beverly Hills with his wife at the time, Gale, with whom I am very close to this day. I lived with my mother during the week and was with my father and Gale only on Sundays. When I turned 13, I finally moved in with him and Gale full time. Living with them gave me a front row seat to the lifestyle business they were thoroughly and passionately engaged in, forging the early dimensions of the entrepreneurial life I would eventually pursue.

Their love for the business was nothing less than a romance. They courted it and enjoyed every part of it, from running the store to handling the merchandise to keeping the books to catering to Hollywood's biggest names to traveling around the world on buying trips. I took care of things in the store from a very early age, cleaning ashtrays, handling deliveries in the shipping department and the bar, and selling clothing to customers.

Watching my father run his business, I never got the sense it was work for him. Rather, I always got the sense my father loved every bit of what he was doing. He and Gale would talk about the business at the dinner table and in the morning over breakfast. They called each other throughout the day to talk about what was going on with the company. They even called my siblings and me to talk about the business. That experience gave me an insider's view about what it was like to really *live* a business. Even though my father and I are very different, I had business in my blood early and knew that one day I would have a business of my own. I didn't know what it would be, but I knew I would have one.

I worked for him until he sold the company to Avon in 1987. Up until then, I thought I would take over for my dad when he could no longer manage the day-to-day operations. The Giorgio fragrance is still around, but the store on Rodeo Drive is gone. In some ways, it's probably better that I didn't step into his shoes, but instead, created companies including Discus Dental, Hayman Advisors, Hayman Properties, and Hayman Ventures that have been a perfect fit for me. That experience has allowed me to have my own identity, something I believe both he and my grandfather encouraged in their respective ways.

My dad had a lot of fine qualities, but one of his best was his ability to be both creative and analytical, drawing on the left and right sides of his brain. While most people tend to be dominant on either the analytical (left) side or the creative (right) side of their brain, my dad was strong in both. He was an innovative visionary, while at the same time having an incredible ability to keep meticulous books for the business. Every record he kept was organized and made sense. He was also extremely generous and gave a lot of money and time to various people and charities.

I consider myself fortunate to have inherited from him the dual ability to be innovative and strategic at the same time. It's not the norm to have both. I've always viewed myself as very creative, but I'm lucky because I can also build a strategy around an idea and see it through. I got that from my father, and it has served me well.

I also inherited his fantastic sense of style and taste. Growing up in the Hayman household, one of the things you learned was manners. If you were at the table, specific rules were in place: keep your elbows by your side, napkin on your lap, mouth closed when you chew your food, sit up straight, don't hunch, and always cut with your right hand and hold the fork with your left.

While he adhered to a certain level of decorum in much of what he did, my father had a great sense of humor and could see the lighter side of life. He was one hell of a funny guy. He knew how to tell jokes, and he understood the fine art of making people feel good about themselves. I've made a point of passing on to my kids the ability to make other people feel good about themselves, too, as well as modeling for them the importance of manners, generosity, a love of good food, having a sense of humor and working hard.

Because of the demands of his business, as well as the way things were back then, my dad didn't spend a lot of time with me the way many fathers spend time with their kids these days. He never came to a football game or a baseball game or a tennis match or a soccer game. It just wasn't part of what he did or who he was. That's one of the reasons I decided to be much more involved with my kids' day to day lives. We eat dinner together as a family, and on the weekends I take them to sports and birthday parties. Even with the demands of running my own businesses, I spend as much time with them as I can, and I don't regret making that choice one bit.

I decided to spend as much time with my father in his later years for similar reasons. I didn't want to miss out or leave things unsaid between us. When he reached his mid-seventies, he began to slow down and eventually developed dementia. I could see he was declining, so as he got older, I made a point of taking him to lunch every Wednesday at Spago, one of his favorite restaurants in Beverly Hills.

I also took him to the symphony, ballet and opera, which he loved dearly. I spent as much time with him as I could and tried to make him feel comfortable. I wanted to learn as much as I could about him and his life, asking him a lot of questions while he could still remember things about his early years. Thankfully, I achieved that goal before he passed away in April 2016 at the age of almost 91. I can honestly say I have no regrets. He lived a great life, and I'm lucky to have been a part of it.

My grandfather was originally from Hungary. He came to America with a desire to work hard and make a life for himself and his family. He had three daughters, and my mom was one of them. He could read and write and he did well, making a reasonable amount of money for his station in life. By Mansfield standards, he was considered successful.

From a young age, I had a very strong connection with him. He was a "man's man" and with a family of only girls, he often called me his son. As a boy, I spent several weeks each summer with him on his farm in Mansfield. One of the earliest memories I have is seeing him through my tears as he stood on the platform in the train station, waving goodbye to me and looking sad as the train pulled away and I headed back home to Beverly Hills. He wanted me to stay and I didn't want to leave. I would have been four or five years old at the time. I loved being with him and followed him like a puppy dog every place he went. Lucky for me, it became a summer tradition.

Following my grandfather around like that was beneficial for me in many ways. Unlike most kids my age who frittered their summers away by the pool or at the beach, I was building the foundation for my future success through learning skills and developing a solid work ethic. Over the years, he taught me how to lay brick, pour concrete, run the tractor, pull a plough through a field, pick strawberries, cut down trees, harvest and split wood.

When we knocked off work around 8 or 9 o'clock each night, it was still sunny. My grandfather was a master storyteller. I remember sitting with him before and after dinner, looking at the fireplace and listening to him tell me story after story after story as he rolled his own smokes. Dust particles and plumes of smoke floated in the air as the sun streamed through the upper window. The house always smelled like a campfire because he used wood for fuel in the winter to keep him and my grandmother warm.

When I was older, we'd have a couple of beers as he smoked and told me more stories. He was kind, honest and understanding, taking his time to explain things to me. He never once disciplined me or ever had harsh words. He modeled life's important values. The time he spent with me meant everything because he filled a void in a way my family wasn't able to fill at the time. His attention gave me the validation I needed as a kid.

One of my funniest memories is when he made a point of correcting my tendency to say too quickly "I know" after he showed me something, which was my way of saying *I got it -- let's move on.*

He'd stop what he was doing, look at me and say, "Oh, so you know, do you? Why don't you tell me all about it, then?"

Calling my bluff, he helped me learn how to think before I responded. He encouraged me to figure things out on my own through trial and error. I caught on fast and learned to slow down, processing what was happening instead of racing on to whatever was next without truly understanding what I was doing. I'm grateful for this lesson as it has served me well in building businesses and raising a family of my own.

High standards like this were part of his character. He expected **nothing but the best** in anything I or anyone else did. He would say, "If you're a bricklayer, be the best damn bricklayer you can be. If you're a janitor, be the best damn janitor you can be. It doesn't matter what you do; just be the best." He drove that principle into me every chance he had, modeling through action how to love what you do and do what you love. And it stuck.

Because of all the time we spent together, we didn't leave anything unsaid. I'd like to think he would be proud of me today. If it were possible, I would love to catch him up on my life, tell him about my kids and my wife, what I'm doing socially and all the organizations I'm a part of. I'd definitely want to say "thank you" for all the time he spent with me, all the life lessons and values he passed on. I'd be sure to let him know I rely every single day on the values he imparted to me. They keep me grounded in a world that can get a bit crazy and, at times, feel unreal.

Because of the examples my grandfather and father set for me, I work hard to set an example for my kids about how to live a great life, too. I don't tell them how to do it; I show them, just like my dad and my grandfather showed me. They never said, "You have to be passionate about your work." They *were* passionate. Each man *lived* his work and showed me by example the true meaning of a life well-lived.

As a result, I don't count the hours I'm at work. I do what I need to do and they add up as they do. The day I start not liking my work is the day I'm not doing it anymore. After all, if you can't expect the best from yourself and what you're doing, how can you possibly expect it from anyone else? If my grandfather and father were here, I think they'd both agree.

Every way of life presents opportunities and challenges, whether you're living on a farm along a gravel road or in a Beverly Hills townhome. Neither one is better nor worse than the other. What makes the difference between a good life and a great one is not so much what you have or don't have, but rather what values and expectations you develop for yourself. I'm fortunate to have experienced being around two very different men who loved me and believed in me in their own unique ways. Men who showed me by example what ultimately matters and what doesn't. Men who made it possible for me to become who I am. At the end of the day, that's arguably the greatest luxury of all.

Behind the Scenes Takeaway

Robert's Skype interview was my last one for the book. We had been trying to coordinate our schedules for six months, but it was definitely worth the wait. His friendliness and sincerity made me feel comfortable as he honored the two men who loved and believed in him in their own, unique ways. During the interview, I enjoyed hearing him laugh out loud as he remembered his grandfather rolling cigarettes and talking about the good people of Mansfield, Ohio, as well as his memories of the legacy of the Hayman family manners. What struck me most about Robert's story was how he could take the best of both his father's and grandfather's lifestyles, work ethics, and personal philosophy of always doing your best no matter what you do in life to ultimately build a life that is uniquely his own. When we can combine the best of the best from those who influence us most, we can architect our lives in ways that matter.

Key Question for Personal Reflection

How have you used the influence of prominent people in your life to build a life that is uniquely your own?

The Noble Mentor

by Ben Osorio

Honoring Dean Franklin

I believe that mentoring is something magical. There are innate, unspoken qualities both parties see in each other. An unspoken understanding and connection exists in the relationship. You appreciate this and because you have that unspoken kind of understanding, you build from there. I also think you have to be noble. You have to know that you're a mentor and then you have to realize that each of you has the other's best interests at heart. I was fortunate to have a mentor like this who put my professional career on the right path. His name was Dean Franklin, and he truly was a **noble mentor.**

Dean was tall and had curly hair. He smiled a lot and always seemed to be happy and at peace with the world. He was also confident, but not in a stern way. I remember him being at ease and self-deprecating. He didn't carry an air about him but modeled what Teddy Roosevelt once said: "Walk softly and carry a big stick." I loved his mannerisms and the fact that at his core, Dean was a good man.

I first met Dean through Elaine, my girlfriend at the time, who would luckily become my wife. I was in my mid-20s working for a savings and loan. I had just completed the fast track program and was working as an Operations Officer in Huntington Park, California. The branch was primarily immigrant, Spanish-speaking and mostly bilingual. The commute was rough, about an hour and 15 minutes one way during good times and longer during bad traffic.

I lived in Canoga Park, which borders Northridge. At the time, my mother was in the final stages of breast cancer. She lived on the other side of the city in Anaheim Hills, which was an additional hour to an hour and a half drive. I was trying to manage my new position and trying to work around her illness. It was a very stressful period, but you learn to manage through those things.

Elaine was working in new accounts for another banking institution. Dean was her manager's husband, and I got to know him while attending functions for Elaine's bank. He and I would chat about business, and I had no idea that, when we were talking, he was secretly interviewing me. I thought our conversations were just open, honest dialogue, just to talk about life. He was in banking, too, and the branch he was in charge of was in a lower-income part of San Fernando. The population was very Hispanic, probably 80 percent Hispanic, and 50 to 60 percent Spanish speaking. Dean knew I was bilingual and with my background, he thought I would be the perfect person to take over that office. Of course, I didn't know he was formulating a plan that included me.

A couple of months later, my mom passed. I transferred to a new branch as a Class I Operations Officer. It was a much smaller, slower branch near where I lived, maybe ten minutes away, which was very convenient. Elaine and I planned on getting married and, to be honest, I was starting to become fairly bored in my role at the bank. With my mind focused on my future, I felt an itch to do something more challenging. I needed to take on things and, like a fish takes to water, I took to banking. It was very simple for me to understand the logic of the banking industry. I had a lot of training in management. It allowed me to touch the many facets of running a business. I was very adept at running the office, and I really wanted to become an assistant manager, with an eye on going into management down the road.

Around this same time marked the beginning of – you can call it an evolution or maybe even a revolution -- when banks were starting to take over other banks. There were consolidations, which were somewhat unheard of back in the day.

My frustration and boredom grew by the day. The company wasn't offering me the kind of upward mobility I wanted, but they were offering other paths to learning more about the banking field. I was asked if I would be willing to go to New York for three months and do a conversion of a state bank. I said "yes" so they bought me a ticket. I was two weeks away from leaving when Dean called me.

He said he had an opportunity for me to manage a branch that required a bilingual manager. It was the worst performing branch he had in his patch, and he thought I would be the perfect person for the job. This is when I realized he'd been interviewing me every time we got a chance to meet.

There's always risk in whatever you do, but I firmly believe opportunity presents itself at the right time. Elaine and I were planning on buying a home. We weren't married yet, but we were buying the house before we were married. Back then, I was so eager. We were very short on cash and income, but we were going to do it anyway. Indirectly, Dean was a lifesaver in the sense that, with this new opportunity, he provided me a salary that allowed us to survive the purchasing process of our new home.

He said, "I would really like you to take it. This is the worst office I have. I need someone who's strong-willed, who has a plan, and who has a clear idea about what he wants to get accomplished. I'm going to let you run the office. You seem to have the skill sets I'm looking for, and I think you have the ability to turn the branch around. Why don't you consider it?"

The confidence and trust he showed in me was inspiring. Of course, it didn't take me long to consider it. I called my branch manager and told her to cancel my ticket to New York.

"I'm not interested in going to New York," I said. "I've been offered another job. I'm going to leave the company."

But I did tell her I was willing to stick around. I didn't want to just leave. I didn't think that was very professional, so I worked the next six weeks and made sure they found someone to replace me. I called Dean and he was willing to accommodate me.

He said, "You know, you're doing the right thing. I like your ethics and your standards. We will wait for you."

Within the first year of working for Dean, I was able to turn that branch from the last place performing branch as a profit center to number one.

Dean believed in what Einstein said about experience -- that experience equals knowledge -- and he let me come up with my own ideas. He never said no, allowing me to run free with what I developed. In return, I lived up to his best expectations.

Dean knew I had a rather in-depth lending background. As a branch manager in one of my previous positions, I was required to sell commercial loans, car loans, and insurance in addition to my regular duties. I even had an insurance license. Turns out, this experience would come in very handy.

When the lending crisis hit in the early 1980s, between '80 and '84, lending basically shut down. Interest rates reached as high as the 20s.

Savings accounts and CDs were being paid out in the 16s and 17s. There was a lot of turmoil with the savings and loan state banks competing against the big commercial banks on the services that were being offered, mutual funds and so forth.

All of a sudden, rates started to drop. They moved from the mid-teens down into the 12s, 11s and 10s, which today you would laugh at, but then it meant everyone wanted to refi. They wanted to get off of the adjustable rates with no limits, no caps, and get at least into something more conservative.

Dean needed to start developing loan officers and he had none to choose from. Everyone was gone. About a year after Elaine and I were married, Dean called me one morning.

"Ben, I'm going to do you a favor," Dean said.

I said, "Dean, I'm open to whatever you need."

He said, "Well, I have to fire you."

This came out of the blue. I said, "Fire me?"

He said, "Yes, but you're going to love the results."

I said, "Dean, I have a house payment. I'm married, no kids yet. I'm really concerned here that this isn't going to work in my favor." (By the way, that year I had a 30 percent bonus on my salary because of all of the goals we'd hit.)

He said, "We'll make things work. We need a lending officer. You have a lot of experience. You will pick up what you need. If you take this job, in a year, I will probably be driving your limo for you."

Thoughts were running through my mind at a lightning pace. *How would I cover the mortgage? What about my family?*

"Give me a day to think about it, Dean," I finally replied.

"I'm going to suggest strongly you take this, Ben," he said. "I wouldn't ask you to do it if I didn't think it was in your best interest."

After hanging up with him, I ran into another mentor, Dave McLaughlin. He's a Scotsman, a character, a brilliant individual.

I said, "You know, Dave, I just got a call from Dean. I'm not sure what to do. I've got a good job, a good salary. I have to worry about what I do for my family."

Dave said, "Well, I got the same call."

I was surprised. "You did?"

"Yeah. He said he wants to shut down the commercial side of lending."

I asked, "So what did you do?"

He said, "Well, I already gave my answer."

"What's that?"

"Come over here."

We walked outside around the corner to the parking lot. He showed me a brand new Mercedes SL.

I said, "What's that for?"

He said, "Well, I took the job and now I have to pay for it. So I'm going to have to work really hard to make it work, aren't I?"

I laughed and he said, "Let me give you some advice. Most people will go the conservative route and not give up the salary because they want the guarantee. A few people will say, I can accept the risk. I will take the risk because I will do much better because it's my responsibility and I trust myself to do it. So if it's for the betterment of your family, why wouldn't you do it?"

At that moment, I had an epiphany. His words really changed my view about assuming risk. I realized: sometimes you need to be conservative, but sometimes you need to be aggressive for the sake of your family's future.

Before I left work that day, I walked back into the office and I told Dean, "Let's do this."

Dean said, "Wonderful."

So I became a loan officer. He gave me a salary. If you were to look at it monetarily after the first year, my salary went up 500 percent from what it had been a year earlier.

During this stage of my career with him, Dean allowed me to make mistakes. He supported me. He gave me a chance to truly become a knowledgeable, professional loan officer. Even after I moved to the lending side of things, he always kept tabs on me and kept all the promises.

When banking became very tumultuous, we lost track of each other. The lending arm of the office I worked for was sold, so Dean moved down another path. But for those three or four years, Dean was instrumental in influencing my success. I was a loan officer for another five to six years, which allowed me the ability to earn enough money to get into my current career as a McDonald's owner-operator.

The skill sets, the interpersonal skills, the human factor skills, the understanding of risk management and finance, all of which I had bits and pieces of before working for Dean, came together under his tutelage. Had it not been for him, I would have probably ended up in a different career completely.

When we would get together at those banking parties for my wife's office and talk about life and business, I was very young. Dean was probably 15 years older than I was. He saw something in me and helped me grow. He didn't see my inexperience as a barrier to whom he wanted. He truly was a wonderful man.

So you can sit outside the story and think, *well Ben, you were just at the right place at the right time and things worked out.* But there are certain subtleties when I look back at that time – especially how Dean managed the relationship with me. When you're young, you can be influenced. Dean just seemed to have an understanding of what needed to be done to allow me to accomplish what I was capable of doing. Obviously, he knew he would also benefit from the decision to bring me on board, but I never sensed he was using me to his benefit, not once. He always looked for the positives.

Dean's skill sets are difficult to find in today's world, or maybe that's what the prior generation's skill set was built on. I think everything is managed so tightly these days. Every movement is dictated through analytics. But you can't measure the human spirit. You can't measure the human factor. You can't measure interpersonal skills or desire. These are skill sets that are still a prerequisite to success, no matter how you categorize it. Dean had that skill set. He never held grudges if something went wrong with someone. He still saw the good in people.

I lost track of Dean because of the commitments it takes to become a McDonald's owner-operator. It's 110 percent. You basically drop your prior life. I relocated from California. Several years ago, I decided to contact Dean but could not locate him. When I finally found his wife, Alice, she told me about his passing.

I told her how much he meant to me and how sorry I was for her loss. I never got a chance to thank him and it was rather sad, but she remembered us.

It's funny. I don't believe you can prescribe mentors. I've learned that being a mentor is somewhat magical, and there's no formula for magic. I've seen leadership that forces mentoring, assigning mentors to people. But it doesn't work like that because nothing is guaranteed. Things can still go wrong. Just like when Dean said, "I can't promise you anything, Ben, but I will do what I can to make it work." He couldn't guarantee it, but he did his best to make it so. In turn, I always did my best to honor him.

Dean was a good man. I think I'm a representation of a lot of what he was. I wish I could hug him and say, "Thank you for your guidance." I think he would probably say, "Ben, you lived up to my best hopes," and I would say, "Dean, you allowed me to."

In the end, what more could you ask than that?

Behind the Scenes Takeaway

When I was interviewing Ben, I noticed he took this opportunity very seriously to honor someone who has impacted his life. Many times he emphasized that his mentor was not only a good man, but also a man of strong character. That really grabbed my attention. One of the biggest takeaways from his story is how mentorship really is an unspoken connection between two people. A lot of elements have to come together for that relationship to work well for both parties. With a foundation of a strong relationship, you have to then trust your mentor to guide you in the best direction. When it works, mentoring can be magnetic.

Key Question for Personal Reflection

From your vantage point, what specific qualities make a mentoring relationship magical?

"We Did It, Pop!"

by Johnny Rutherford

Honoring John Sherman Rutherford, Jr.

If you don't go to the edge and look over once in a while, life gets boring. That's what racing is about. Going to that edge and seeing just how far down it is, how close you can get.

The racing bug bit me young. I have my Dad, John Sherman Rutherford, Jr., to thank for that. He was adventurous, having served in the Air Force until he retired and became a Warrant Officer in 1949. I grew up around airplanes and race cars and boats, watching Dad do everything. He fixed cars. He fixed boats. He fixed things in our house. He really was Mr. Fix It.

When we lived in Coffeyville, Kansas, we didn't have a garage. Dad borrowed the garage from the house across the street and took a 19-foot, Chris-Craft runabout he was servicing for someone and turned it upside down. The bottom and the sides of those boats are mahogany planking. Dad used a wide chisel and rope caulking between the boards to seal up the spaces between the planks.

He was one of the best mechanics of aircraft engines anyone had ever seen. People said you could fire up an engine, and he could listen to it and be able to tell what was wrong. When they'd tear it down, sure enough, what my dad said was wrong was, indeed, what was wrong.

I picked up some of his abilities. I have him to thank for my mechanical inclinations. They would come in handy when I built my first race car years later. I had help, of course, but I drew on Dad's influence to get the job done.

He was also a tremendous swimmer, a state champion. One time, Johnny Weissmuller came to Coffeyville. Johnny was the man who played Tarzan in the movies. He offered to race anybody who wanted to.

Dad said, "I'll race you" and he beat Johnny!

I didn't need a movie star to look up to.

Dad was my hero.

Dad took me to my first midget car race when I was nine years old. World War II had just ended. Racing fans everywhere were hungry for entertainment because the war had put a halt on sports like racing. It was a Saturday night at the fairgrounds in Tulsa. To see the chrome glinting on those brightly colored midget cars going around the quarter mile dirt track was really something.

What I remember most about going to the race track that first time was the energy of the fans. Up to four to five thousand people came to the track at once. The Tulsa fairgrounds had a huge, wooden grandstand and a built-in, one-mile track where horses had run before racing big cars became popular. A quarter mile track was in front of the grandstand where the midget cars ran. I couldn't go into the pits until after the race because I was too young, but Dad went into the pits because he was a steward and was rallying cars for the races, lining them up for each heat.

As a 9-year old, I sat in the stands and watched the midget cars run. The fans cheered for their favorites and oohed and ahhed when there was an incident. I could feel the electricity in the air. It was exciting when the cars lined up and got ready to go. Lloyd Ruby was running in Tulsa then. I can remember the announcers saying, "And now...going out to qualify... ladies and gentlemen...the young man from Wichita Falls, Texas...a star in the making...19-year-old...Lloyd Ruby!"

Lloyd Ruby was a really great race car driver, always dead on the mark. Later, when I entered the racing circuit, I knew going into a heat Lloyd would be one of my competitors. He and I became friends over the years, and he helped me get into my first race at Indianapolis in 1963. I'll never forget what he said to me just as I was firing up and getting ready for my qualifying run for the Indianapolis 500.

He leaned over the driver's side and said, "Ruuutherford..." (he talked really slow -- and he didn't call me Rutherford, he called me "Rollllll-lerford") "Rollllllerford, don't let us Texans down!"

You better believe I did everything I could not to.

After my first experience at the fairgrounds with Dad, everything I did had something to do with racing. I remember going out to the guard hangar in Tulsa with Dad. It was the 125th fighter squadron of P 51 Mustangs, and I got to climb all over them. Dad told me what not to touch, and then I would pretend to be a fighter pilot and a race car driver.

One time, Dad bought a midget race car. His buddies on the guard base pushed him down the road. He drove it for a stretch and then came back. Those midget race cars have locked rear ends with their spider gears welded up. Dad was trying to go back through the gate at the guard base and the road was gravel. When he turned the car in, the front end of the car pushed like a pig and went straight, hitting the corner post. He was thrown forward and cut his nose up the side.

When he came home, my mother Doris was not pleased.

She said, "You're not going to do that anymore!"

And he had the sense to hire a driver to drive the midget from then on.

My mother went to only one race with me in Tulsa. I sat with her in the stands, watching the race. As the cars were coming around turn four to start the heat race, one of them got over one of the other cars. The wheels jammed with the other car and it flipped right in front of us. The driver was killed. That was the end of my mother going to the races. She was completely against me becoming a race car driver.

Mom would say, "You don't want to be a racetrack bum." It was her way of trying to get me to change my mind.

Back then, racetrack mechanics wore greasy t-shirts and had dirty fingernails. Things have come a long way since, but she was not in favor of me becoming someone like that. Going to the races divided our house, becoming a story that was always running in the background. Dad supported me, while my mother remained fiercely against my dream.

Dad finally told her: "You either join him or you lose him because Johnny is going racing, no matter what."

Mom came around to my racing eventually. After Dad said we either join him or lose him, she figured that's what it was, and she wasn't going to change it.

I don't think it hurt any when I won the Indianapolis 500 for the first time several years later.

But to get to the Indianapolis 500, I needed help beyond what Dad had taught me. I built my first car while I was a member of the local Idlers hot rod club in River Oaks, Texas. At a meeting one night, one of the guys came in and said he needed to leave early to help his brother put the engine into his dirt track car.

That sat me straight up in my chair. I said, "Dirt track car?"

He said, "Oh yeah. They race every Friday night over at the Devil's Bowl Speedway in Dallas."

So the next day, I went out with him to test run the car. I probably should have stopped by the doctor's office first and gotten a tetanus shot because, back then, they were open-wheel cars. They didn't have a body on the car, just the frame and roll cage.

After that trip to the Devil's Bowl, I immediately divested myself of anything I could get money for and found a 1932 Chevrolet coupe in Grapevine at a shutdown service station. I bought it then towed it back to the clubhouse on Robert's Cutoff Road. The president of the club had a garage with a dirt floor, and I put the car in there and got started building my first race car.

With help from the guys in the club, I had my first ride on the Dallas dirt track in my own car in April 1959.

Dad wasn't able to watch me race in Dallas at the Devil's Bowl, but he did make some trips later in my career when I got into sprint cars, running the fair circuit. He always supported my dream of racing. He knew the dangers of the sport. But when you're young and feeling like a hot dog, you don't see it as dangerous. Bad things happen to everyone else, not you. Dad made the trip up to Dayton, Ohio, in 1966 where I was in the hospital with two broken arms and a severe concussion. He wanted to see if I was going to make it. It was hard for him to travel and see me regularly. He did the best he could.

Learning the things you have to learn to be a race car driver is like learning anything else. You learn the feel of the car, what you do to make the car change in its attitude and handling. It's all part of the big learning curve you have from the beginning of your career until you retire. And it's such a wonderful feeling -- I call it a smiling moment -- when you figure something out and it works. Another thing I picked up from Dad.

I started racing my car at the Devil's Bowl, which was pretty primitive compared to the hot dogs I raced against. But it was a start. It was 1959, and I made friends with one of the top drivers at the Devil's Bowl, Jim McElreath. He had his own car and was one of the leaders of that era. Jimmy had plans to graduate and go up into the Midwest and get into **big time** racing.

Mid-season 1960, I took my car to the track and sold it to someone who made it their burner. I got $180 for it, less the engine. For 1960, that wasn't too bad.

Shortly after that, Jimmy and I left Texas and drove straight up to Milwaukee, Wisconsin. There was a twin 50 USAC sprint car race there at the fairgrounds on the mile. The track was paved! Jimmy knew some people up there and I knew some people I'd met through racing. He already had plans to race at Lawrenceburg, Indiana, and Eldora Speedway in Ohio, along with a couple of other tracks in the area. He had a super modified car to drive for a big contractor in Covington, Kentucky, right across the river from Cincinnati.

Eventually, we both secured sprint cars to drive on the fair circuit. I doubt if you could name a state or county fair in the Midwest with a half mile dirt track where they run sprint cars that I haven't been on. The last year I raced IMCA (International Motor Contest Association), I ran 73 races in one summer. The World of Outlaws does a lot more than that now, but back then, 73 races was a lot.

It would become the foundation for my career at Indy.

1963 came around. This was the first year I would race at Indy, and it was also the year I met my wife Betty, who would become my rock and biggest fan. She was a registered nurse and was working at the speedway on her days off from the hospital. She let me have the freedom to pay attention to what I was doing and trying to get better at it. As my career soared, she took over the house and kids. She went to every race with me, never once wavering from her commitment to me and my pursuits.

I was having trouble with the car I was driving for the qualifying run for the Indianapolis 500. The chief mechanic (whose name was Buster Warke and would become a dear friend) was in the garage trying to set the car up. It was primitive. There were four grain scales. Buster would jack the car up and put the grain scales under the wheels to measure the car's corner weight. This system could get the weights right, but the heights would be off. It could also get the heights right, but the weights would be off. Buster determined the chassis had a tweak in it somewhere, so we couldn't dial it to the finest degree.

Buster said, "Why don't you walk down the line and see if you can find something else you could drive? Take a comparison ride and see what you think?"

So I walked down the line and ran into a friend named Eddie Kostenec. Eddie had one of the leader car Watson Roadsters, which was one Roger Ward had driven. It was a good race car. A rookie driver from California was in it and he was struggling.

I said, "Eddie, could I take a ride in your car?"

He said, "Sure."

My friend Lloyd wasn't far away and Eddie said, "Lloyd drove it yesterday. Maybe he can tell you something about it."

Lloyd said, "This is a good race car. I would drive it in the race. But I'll tell you one thing. When it goes down in the corner, and you feel it bump that curb, just get after the throttle. It'll take it."

I ran six laps with it. When I got back to the pit, I pulled in and it stopped. Eddie was running around and I could see the other guys getting things ready. I got out of the car and they pushed it away.

I said, "Well, I must not have done very good."

And Eddie said, "Oh no. They're just going to get fuel. You're going to qualify!"

This would be the first car I would run Indy in.

I was a graduate of sprint cars, racing dirt and pavement. A sprint car doesn't teach you how to run at Indianapolis. But it darn sure teaches you how to race. Sprint car racing is wheel to wheel, 120 mile per hour flat-chat-go-for-it-pitch-it-in-the-corner and know just how far you can go. It's a great instructor.

I remember what Lloyd told me once: "Feel the car bump that curb and get after it. You can do that when you hit that curb and you feel it and you hit it just right. You're a little ahead of it, maybe, then you're going fast enough and you have enough drift in the car when you feel that the car jumps it and does a whip."

In the third turn on my third lap qualifying, there were two drivers sitting on the observer's stand between the third and fourth turn. Johnnie Boyd and Bob Veith. They were watching the cars qualify. I came into turn three and got after it, trying to get that extra little bit. Just as the car bumped the curb, I could see out of my peripheral vision Boyd and Veith diving off of the stand. They figured I was going to nail the wall and they didn't want to get any of the pieces flying their direction.

But I made the race. It was gratifying, but I was also surprised. I remember thinking, "Wow, is that all there is to it?"

When I got through the four phases of my test, I took the ritual three tape stripes off the tail of my car. I had passed! At that point, I was allowed to use all of the race track. I could run as fast as I wanted to. During the first three qualifying phases, drivers can only use half of the race track because they weren't going as fast. But on the fourth phase, drivers get to use the rest of the race track.

So I went back out there and got in the groove. I felt like Roger Ward or Troy Rutman. Turns out, Ward joined on the track at turn two down the backstretch. I had already gone by. Back then, the roadsters didn't have mirrors and I made the lap and came around the back stretch. Roger Ward went by me like I was painted on the fence. Sucked my goggles out about three feet from my face. That's when I thought, "What in the hell am I doing here?"

It was an awakening. I realized, *there's a little more to this than just the testing*. I'd have to work on the speed. Unfortunately, the car sprung an oil leak and put us out of the race. But I sure learned a lot that day back in 1963.

When God reaches in your book and tears your page out, it's over.

I knew Dad was sick when I raced at Indy in 1974. He would pass away not long after that at age 61. His prostate cancer had metastasized into his bones. He was in a lot of pain.

Still, he watched the race on television. Mom told me later it was the last thing he ever watched. I dedicated my race to him, looking at the camera and saying, **"We did it, Pop!"**

He went straight to bed afterwards and that was about it. The demands on my time after winning Indianapolis were horrendous. Thankfully, we had a chance to talk in his final days. It was good for me and it was good for Mom. I was able to let him know how much he meant to me. I'm so grateful he got to see me when I won my first Indy 500.

Dad was proud of me and my accomplishments. He admired the tenacity with which I attacked my career. Dad's life was aviation and his hobby was race cars. My life was race cars and my hobby is aviation. It's funny how things work out like that.

When I think about the people who influenced me throughout my life, I see a clear pattern. Dad helped me start my career. Jimmy McElreath, Lloyd Ruby and many others helped me refine it. Betty helped me survive it. Much of the camaraderie we shared was expressing how grateful we were for the help, guidance, and support we gave to each other. We enjoyed each other's company and we respected each other's accomplishments. In many ways, we went to the edge together. One person's win was everyone's win, and we were all the better for it.

Behind the Scenes Takeaway

When interviewing Johnny, it was magical watching him describe his love for the fans. He appreciated the way they loved the sport, and he got energy from them to keep going even when times were tough or discouraging. One of my biggest takeaways from Johnny's story is the importance of having permission from those closest to us for success in life. As a child, Johnny had raw talent and skills. Because of his dad's support, the equation for success was complete.

Key Question for Personal Reflection

Think about a time when the power of others fueled your own aspirations and you were able to accelerate your career, goals, or life forward.

The Ride through Two Worlds

by Krista Dabakis Price

Honoring Shirley Palmer

Being a teenager can be rough in any era, but the early 1970s were especially crazy. I was in junior high school at that time, with the Vietnam War, rock n roll music, and the cultural revolution as the backdrop to my formative years. It was a turbulent time, and my choices to live in two worlds only added fuel to the fire.

On the one hand, I was the president of my church's youth group, where people saw me as a leader and a role model. On the other, I was hanging around the cool kids who weren't heading in the right direction, doing things I shouldn't have been doing. Living in two worlds, I found myself at a crossroads. Had it not been for Shirley Palmer, it's hard to say how things would have turned out for me.

It was a strange time trying to balance who I was. I'm not sure how much she knew about my wild side, but none of that ever seemed to matter to her. When I jumped in her car to have our little ride to and from church, everything else disappeared. For twenty minutes it was as if I was on **a ride through two worlds** where life was good and everything seemed possible.

Shirley lived near me and was involved in the church's youth group. She didn't know my family well, but she knew of my brothers and sisters and eventually came to know me the best. I wanted to join the youth group at my church, but my parents didn't go to church, so Shirley picked me up and drove me home every Sunday. During our drive, we had insightful conversations about everything from how the Red Sox were doing to how school was going to what I planned to do when I grew up. If there was a Red Sox game on, we listened to it. If there was something going on at home or church, we talked about it. She taught me the art of conversation, which is something I carry with me to this day.

The time in the car I had with Shirley was consistently positive and upbeat. Each week, I looked forward to the ride to and from church with her. Life at home was rough. My mom struggled with emotional issues, and my dad did his best to hold us all together. We didn't have family meals, and we certainly didn't have conversations around a table, or anywhere else for that matter. Shirley showed me life didn't have to be like the way my mother's life was. She gave me a different lens to look through, and she always treated me like I had a head on my shoulders with valid ideas and thoughts to contribute. Having a conversation where what I had to say was as important as what she had to say was a new experience for me. I liked that.

Shirley was from Maine and had a strong Maine accent. I liked to listen to her talk. We lived in Massachusetts and we were both Red Sox fans, so we talked a lot about the games and the team. The Red Sox never did well when I was growing up. Even when the Red Sox were losing, which was often, Shirley maintained a cheerful outlook about their potential. She always found something good about the team's performance. She was the same way toward me and everyone else she interacted with.

She had no children of her own, and her husband was in a wheelchair. He had either multiple sclerosis or muscular dystrophy and was in pretty bad shape. He eventually died and she had plenty of reasons to not be so rosy all the time. But even in the face of great loss and heartbreak, her attitude remained upbeat and positive.

Indeed, she never talked about negative things. Even though I was young, I had a sense about the world. I knew it wasn't always a nice place. Yet no matter what, Shirley stayed positive. She seemed oblivious to the bad stuff. It could have had something to do with her New England stoicism. She never gushed over people or things. Or it could have been because she sang in a couple of choirs. I think singing helped keep her young. Or maybe she was just made that way, with an extra helping of positivity.

I was lucky to be the beneficiary of her kind-heartedness. We had an understanding between us, even though I wasn't always so thoughtful towards her. Once we got to church, for example, I was into my friends and didn't have much to do with her. She wouldn't have expected anything less of me, though. She treated me as if I was a great person and a great leader, no matter what.

Everything Shirley did was subtle. There was no overt teaching or lessons held up high. This could be why I learned a lot in those trips. Don't dwell on the negative things was one of the biggest lessons she taught. There's always something positive. She was always rock steady, a leveling, positive force in my life. I don't think I knew I was learning these lessons at the time. But when I look back at that time in my life, I realize I learned a lot from her.

I don't know if she knows what kind of impact she had on me. I saw her recently when I traveled back for my father's funeral. I hadn't seen her in a long time. I couldn't wait for her to meet my kids. It was wonderful to see her. She had not changed a bit. She's in her eighties now, but she did not look all that different. She aged well. She has the same haircut; she has a bit of the New England accent. Her outlook on the world is as positive today as it was when I was a teen.

To this day, I have a soft spot for teenagers. Even though my teaching career didn't lead me to work with that age group, I really like to be around adolescents. I love when my college-age son brings 3-4 friends home for the weekend. They'll all sleep in the living room and go hiking the next day. I respect them and believe their opinions matter, just like Shirley believed in me and my opinions. There's more to teenagers than most people give them credit for, and Shirley helped me see that.

I hope I have a little bit of Shirley in me today, in my character and how I treat people and how I talk to them and afford them dignity. If I were to thank her today, I would want her to know how influential she was to me. She's the type of person that doesn't live her life to impress anybody or be an example. She just is. She's true to herself and shows up that way in all situations.

Shirley was a consistent force in my life. If she knew how much of an influence she was on me, I think she'd be a bit embarrassed, downplaying her role in shaping me. But I also think it would make her very happy.

Behind the Scenes Takeaway

When I was interviewing Krista, I could sense the gratitude she had for Shirley and her consistent force through this confusing stage in Krista's life. Shirley's positive outlook seemed so contagious. I can only imagine the conversations they had during their 20-minute car rides. Shirley made Krista feel valued and important, gifts you can't buy. One of the biggest takeaways from her story is being a teenager is hard, but even more so when there are challenges at home. Most teenagers are searching for their identity, and sometimes it's not the most obvious person who steps in with a positive message and fills a void that, in turn, opens up possibilities they never knew existed.

Key Question for Personal Reflection

Who have you known – either personally or observed from a distance – that is a "rock steady, leveling, positive force?" What have they done specifically that you would want to model?

The Revelation

by Katherine Jones

Honoring the One Within

Unlike a lot of people who can point to one particular mentor or influence, I never had one specific person who believed in me. Rather, my personal transformation came out of circumstances and events I experienced over the years, leading me to develop what I now call my internal guidance system. But even that didn't happen until I was fifty-five years old, when I really began to live the life I was meant to live.

I've come to understand that the people I've known throughout my life were put here to challenge me so I could find my higher self and become the best version of me. I have always said my oldest daughter came into my life to save my life, and my youngest daughter came into my life to challenge my life. I've always wanted to be the mother I didn't have, but there's no manual or guidance system about how to be the best mom, especially not at 17. I sure didn't know what I was doing, but I muddled through, making a lot of mistakes along the way.

I got married at 16, had my first daughter at 17, and before I was 18, that marriage was over. I was devastated, of course -- it was like a dagger in my heart when it ended. For a while, I got caught up in the world of just surviving, doing my best to move on from the pain.

By the time I turned 19, I was already remarried with another child. I'd moved to the Dallas-Fort Worth area and settled into family life. I'd been a dancer since I was three years old, and I continued to dance until my mid-twenties. My oldest daughter Candie and I went to ballet when she got old enough. She attended a beginning class and I was in the advanced.

It's amazing how fast the years went by. Before I knew it, my kids were grown and gone. Then my husband passed away after a long illness and I became a caregiver for my mother. She and I didn't have any kind of mother-daughter relationship whatsoever. I worked more than 60 hours a week and was on the road a lot for my career. I never got a break, and I was exhausted. To cope, I started drinking heavily. I had always been a social drinker -- I could take it or leave it, but around the time I turned 50 and my world felt like it was unraveling, alcohol became something I needed to get through the day, instead of an occasional way to unwind or celebrate.

It wasn't long before I'd become a functional alcoholic. I was making things in my life much bigger than they were, falling into a drama trap at every turn. I was also full of self-pity; it felt like I had done so much for so many and all they were doing was turning their backs on me. With my self-pity running rampant, I drank even more.

Eventually, I went into complete isolation. I quit eating. I got dangerously thin. Then I got to a point where I couldn't keep anything down. I just didn't care anymore. My kids had quit talking to me because I was so full of anger and resentment. Yet in my mind I was saying, "Nobody cares, you know, nobody cares." The truth was, I'd stopped caring about myself. It would take a near-death experience to make me finally see how off course I'd gone.

The day I nearly died, my brother arrived in Fort Worth from Atlanta for a business trip. My brother and I weren't close at the time, and he still doesn't know what compelled him to call me that day when he got to the DFW airport. I believe divine intervention was at work. Only a few days before coming to Fort Worth, he and a coworker had been talking and my brother had said to this guy, "Have you ever wondered what your purpose is? Sometimes I just kind of go, why am I even really here?" My brother tends to keep to himself, and he doesn't know why he said anything to this guy because he wasn't a friend -- just more of an acquaintance. Lo and behold, a few short days later, he would save my life -- and know his purpose.

I didn't know he was coming to town and I don't have any memory of him telling me he was coming to town, but he called when he landed and when I didn't answer the phone, something made him rent a car and drive to my house. I didn't answer the door, either, because as it turns out, I had collapsed and was laid out on the ground.

My brother was sure I was dead. This is a guy who does not cry, yet when he tells this story, tears roll down his face. As an engineer, he says by all rights I should have been dead, given the circumstances. When the paramedics got there, they said I was clinically dead, but they revived me with epinephrine and the paddles, not knowing how long I'd been out. Apparently, I was still warm. They took me to Baylor Hospital and I have no memory of being in intensive care. Later, I learned the doctors had told my daughters, "Your mother will more than likely wind up in a nursing home for the remainder of her life."

It was determined I had been in a semi-coma for five days or so before I collapsed. When I came to, I looked around the hospital room wondering, "Where am I? What's going on?"

Suddenly a buzzer was going off and a nurse came running in. She hit the call button and said, "She's back! She's back!"

I looked at her and said, "What am I doing here?" I had a big smile on my face. I felt so calm.

The doctor came in the room and told me what day and time it was.

I said, "You have that all wrong. This is the date and this is what time it is."

When they insisted I was confused, I became agitated, telling them, "I need to go back to where I was. I don't think I belong here. I really need to go back."

The nurse and the doctor looked at each other, raising their eyebrows. I'm sure they see that kind of stuff in ICU all the time with patients who have had near-death experiences. They said I was hallucinating, but I know what hallucinating is like and this was not a hallucination.

When I talked to my daughter Candie for the first time after the incident, she said, "Mom, you need some help."

I said, "I know, isn't it wonderful?"

At this point, Candie was bracing herself for a fight with me because that's normally what I would do.

But instead of fighting with her, I said calmly, "You know what? There is nothing I can't do in this life. There's nothing I can't do."

Candie wasn't sure what to make of that comment. This was not the mom she knew. To this day, she'll say, "You know, there was something about when you were in the hospital and you said those words, 'I can do anything.' It just resonated with you, Mom, and you haven't gone back on that."

That was seven years ago, and she's right. My near-death experience made me feel completely free -- and the feeling hasn't changed. As part of my new-found freedom, I've decided to move to be close to my daughter and grandchildren. Of course, there have been times since then when I've felt depression creeping back, thinking I was too old to restart my life. But this is also the time when the connection with my higher power really started, and it's honestly what has kept me going and changed the direction of my life.

I have an intense memory from my childhood that explains a lot about my belief system. I knew nothing about religion or spirituality. According to what I was taught in church, the God I was told about was a very judgmental God. I no longer believe that, but it definitely influenced my childhood.

One night, when I was six or seven years old, I woke up with the feeling like something was trying to crush my head. I was terrified, so I went into my mother's room.

I said, "Can I get in bed with you?"

I was crying. I had never asked to do that before.

She said, "I got to work tomorrow. Go back to bed."

I went back to my room and sat on my bed, shaking. I knew I needed help, so I started talking to God through my tears because I knew He wasn't all bad. I knew He loved to help me, too.

That was my first experience calling on the God within to help me get through a hard time. I felt God saying, "You don't have to worry about this." That's when I developed the *I've got to take care of myself* attitude, because no one else was going to. I'd been introduced to my inner strength.

After leaving the hospital, I realized I couldn't continue traveling for work, or deal with the heavy stress of taking care of everyone else. I took a year and all I did was focus on calming myself down and strengthening my connection to my higher self. I started reading every book I could find on near death experiences and quickly discovered each one is unique in its own right.

A common theme for people who nearly die and then come back is a feeling of going through a tunnel. There was no tunnel for me. What I experienced was very well lit, but it wasn't the kind of blinding light that hurts your eyes. It also wasn't lit by any sun.

During my time being gone, I felt like I was in a cocoon, not on this earth, surrounded with love. All I could feel was love, love, and more love. I remember hearing music and seeing a lot of children who were happy --

very, very happy. I truly believe the light was healing me of all the trauma I'd had in my life, allowing me to work on my relationships. Growing closer to my brother. Becoming a more caring mother to my daughters. Becoming a more caring daughter instead of a resentful daughter.

I distinctly remember the moment I pulled up to my mother's nursing home a few months into my self-healing. It was a cool day, and it was brisk. I turned off the ignition and sat in my car, looking at the sun.

I said, "God, you've got this." And I knew He did.

When I walked into the nursing home, I felt completely different than I ever had before. I felt confident. I felt strong. In my old life, I would have rewarded myself for visiting my mom in the home by getting a bottle of wine afterwards. That's when alcohol became a crutch for me. I didn't need that crutch anymore.

One of the other things I discovered soon after my near-death experience is I no longer have to have all the answers -- and it's okay. In my old life, I saw myself as an information source. That's what I did for a living. As a mother, that's how I would handle things. As a wife, I always said, "This is what you need to do and when you need to do it." I'll never forget the first time somebody asked me a question after I got out of the hospital and I said, "I don't know. What do you think?" It was a revelation.

Now when things don't go the way I think they should, I pause and ask myself, "I wonder what this means? I wonder what's next?" instead of, "Holy crap! What the Hell is going on here?" I'm able to accept the unknown because inside myself, I'm 100% confident about the knowing and how it influences my everyday life: to love what is going on, to love it for what it is because there is a reason. Do I get off kilter? Absolutely. Do I get all up in my head? Absolutely. I'm a spirit having a human experience. It's part of the deal.

I also believe the only reason I came back was because I needed to live my life differently, from a place of love and understanding instead of anger and resentment. Over the course of two to three years afterwards, I talked to other near death experiencers, almost as a way of validating what happened to me. I've asked myself many times, *Did that really happen?* Some people I've talked to say the same thing happens to them. You start feeling like you're getting sucked back into your previous life after a number of years have passed.

But I'll never get sucked back into the life I had before. I actually go out of my way these days to avoid chaos and drama. But if things start to get crazy, I recoil from the drama like it's a hot flame. It doesn't belong to me. What other people are thinking of me or anyone else is really none of my business.

Instead, I practice gratitude. In fact, practicing gratitude is an integral part of my day, every day. What's interesting about this is, when I first started making a gratitude list, it started off with things like, "Oh I'm grateful for my paid-off car. I'm grateful for my home. I'm grateful for my children. I'm grateful for all this stuff." Now, I find myself saying, "I'm grateful for my relationship with my higher power. I'm grateful for the unconditional love and guidance of my higher power." All this stuff I used to put on the list isn't there anymore. Instead, my gratitude has to do with the feelings in my life. It has to do with being shown what direction to go. It has to do with the people in my life, like my brother. I'm grateful for him every day. And that's a huge shift for me.

Another shift I've had is in my career. I now professionally help people who are recovering from addiction. I'm able to help people in a way I never would have been able to without going through all the trauma that led up to nearly dying. In fact, that experience has everything to do with the work I do now. I love what I do, because I'm helping people who are the way I used to be. I understand their pain and their struggles, and I let them be who they are on their way to who they can become.

But there is a hitch to my work, and it took me a while to see it: you can only give back to someone who really wants it. You can't force your purpose onto someone else. In the beginning, I wanted to shout from the rooftops and try to save everyone. Now, I accept people where they are, knowing they have to walk their own path, just like I did. And for me, that's **the greatest revelation of all.**

Behind the Scenes Takeaway

When I was interviewing Kathy, I could feel her sense of freedom as she recalled how she came to live a life that matters to her. One of the biggest takeaways from her story is it's okay to not have all the answers all the time. By letting go of trying to be in control in every situation, we become available to new experiences and deeper relationships with others as well as ourselves. I admire Kathy for using her experience as a way to help others find their own way.

Key Question for Personal Reflection

How has a profound experience in your life helped you discover your purpose and, in turn, made a difference to others?

Family First

by John Lopez

Honoring Victor and Connie Lopez,
and Herman Gallegos

The American Dream is often measured by how much money a person makes and the material things a person owns. People from all over the world continue to come to this country to pursue their dream of a better economic life. While money and material things are nice, they don't complete the dream and aren't the ultimate measure of how successful a person is. I've been blessed with fulfilling my American Dream and the rewards money can buy. But none of what I own is as important to me as my family. In fact, I could not have attained my business success without the combination of hard work, sacrifice, a great family, and the right mentor. Had it not been for the example of my parents, Victor L. and Concepcion "Connie" Salinas Lopez, the steadfast love and support of my wife Pat, or the wisdom and example of my first business mentor, Herman Gallegos, I would not have achieved the goal of becoming a millionaire, a goal I shared with a friend one night in college over a few beers.

If my parents were the pool where I learned to swim with the values of hard work, fidelity, and loyalty, then my mentor Herman Gallegos was the springboard that catapulted me into the deep end of business success where I have been swimming ever since. There have been others who have influenced me along the way, but my parents set me up for success in my childhood, and Herman Gallegos solidified it for me as a young man searching for the way to achieve my goal of financial freedom. Pat has filled in the gaps everywhere else, reminding me every day, "You could only do this with your wife beside you, not behind you." No truer words have ever been spoken.

I got a solid start with my entrepreneurial education at home watching Mom and Dad run their own business. They were a success story in themselves. They were both farm workers with aspirations for a better life. Dad's family was in the mining industry in eastern Arizona. Dad was the oldest and was mining with his brothers and my paternal grandfather when they decided to move to the Valley of the Sun for grandpa's health. That's where my dad met my mom.

My maternal grandfather was also an entrepreneur. His name was George Salinas and he had a trucking company called the Salinas Trucking Company. He hauled cantaloupe and watermelon and baled hay for the farmers in the Glendale, Arizona, area. I suspect that's where my mom got her entrepreneurial traits from.

After my parents got married, they continued working on farms and for grandpa until my dad decided he wanted a better job. He found a part-time position as a butcher at a grocery store in Glendale. He learned how to be a butcher, but he also learned the grocery business, which he taught to me and my siblings. Ten years later, he owned the grocery store. Grandpa financed him. And Mom and Dad officially became entrepreneurs.

I had to work in the morning and help Dad open the store and sweep and clean it up, so he could continue doing business throughout the day. I had to set up the produce area. After school in the evenings, I had to return to the store and help clean, stock up cans, pack five and ten-pound bean bags, and lock up the store for the night. On the weekends, I worked all day Saturday from seven in the morning until nine o'clock at night and Sundays from seven in the morning until one in the afternoon. My parent's expectation to help with the store established my work ethic. It was hard, and I didn't always enjoy it. But I believe my experience working in my family's grocery store formed a cornerstone of my future success.

What also influenced me was seeing my parent's dedication to their store and applying themselves to the business. I could see their passion for it. I could see when they were starting to feel successful and they wanted to pass that on to their children. They taught us what it took to really make it in business. It wasn't so much what they said, but what they did that made an impression on me.

I was a 14-year old young man, running a cash register, dealing with numbers, putting money on a voucher because my dad offered credit to a lot of people who bought groceries for the week and came back at the end of the week to pay their bill, then start another bill for the following week. I saw how money was used and transferred, how loyal people were to my parents, and how loyal my parents were to their customers. I learned how important it is to be loyal to your customers, know who they are, what they want, and what you can do to help them. That's one of the greatest lessons I continue to draw on today.

I also learned that they didn't make money and then put it away just for themselves; they shared what they earned. My mother showed me how to plan. She was great at thinking about the future, always six or seven months ahead of my dad when it came down to what they were going to be doing. My dad was great at the day-to-day and week-to-week operations of running a business. Because of them, I know what I'm doing hour-by-hour and day-by-day in my businesses, and I also know where I am going to be in the next 10 years.

The only time Mom and Dad allowed me and my siblings to have time off was either when we were in sports or when we were involved with church. So I played football, baseball, and became an altar boy in church because that meant I had to go to mass and devote more of my "free" time to something outside of working in the store. Not that I wanted to avoid working at the grocery store, but I figured out I didn't like being tied down to that rigorous schedule. I simply needed a break! Sports and church gave me that outlet while teaching me other valuable lessons about life that I would use in my future entrepreneurial ventures.

I was very proud of my parents. They were recognized in our community. My father was the first Latino City Councilman in the city of Glendale, Arizona. One of three in the entire state. My mother was a driving force behind my dad. He would have been happy wearing khaki pants and a white tee shirt, smoking cigarettes and drinking beer with the guys. But Mom wouldn't let him do that. Mom pushed him, saying, "We have kids. We have values. We want to educate our children. We need to earn income to do that." Watching him, I learned how to be a good father and devoted family man when it was time to raise children of my own.

I also learned about setting goals from Mom and Dad. One of their biggest goals in life was to get out of the fields and do better for their children through business ownership so they could educate all of their children. My older brother got a degree and became a coach and a teacher. My younger brother graduated from Northern Arizona University and became a banker. My parents fully expected me to follow in my older brother's footsteps and become a teacher and coach, too.

But I was not built to be that type of a coach or a teacher, and I would ultimately get my education outside of a college setting. After I lost my football scholarship at NAU due to a shoulder injury, I dropped out of school and entered the banking industry where my "formal" business education began. My parents weren't thrilled with the direction I was taking my life, but without my scholarship, I had no other options. Pat and I were married at this point with a baby girl on the way. I had to do something to support my growing family. I liked the idea that bankers were around money. I liked the idea that they dressed up in suits and ties.

It was about this same time when I went out for a couple of beers with a good friend of the family. His name was Louis Reyna.

We got to talking about the future, and I said, "Louis, you're a senior in college. You're going to graduate soon. What are you going to do?"

He said, "John, I am so happy! I'm going to go teach and coach back in my home community. I've got some job offers already. I'm going to make the world go round. I want to do what our coaches have done for us here at ASC. How about you?"

I said, "I want to be a millionaire! I'm going to be a millionaire!"

His jaw dropped and he said, "How are you going to do that?"

"I don't know," I said. "What I do know, though, is that is going to be my goal."

So I wrote it down. Somehow, putting it in writing made it more real.

One day, I will be a millionaire.

I quickly realized banking wasn't going to get me there. I thought I would work from 8-5, five days a week and then be at home. But the reality of life, the reality of expenses, the reality of raising a family with a third daughter by then forced me to take a look at what banking was doing for me. Yes, it became a foundation for my education. It gave me an inside look at bank operations, financing, and what makes the world tick. It also exposed me to clients who were entrepreneurial and small business owners like my dad and mom had been. I didn't have a mentor and I was living paycheck to paycheck. I needed to do something to really get ahead.

That's when I got a call from Armando DeLeon that would change my life forever.

Armando DeLeon was a young City Councilman who had just been elected in Phoenix, Arizona. Armando was on the board of directors of a group called the Southwest Council of La Raza (SWCLR). It was a program funded by the Ford Foundation to help Latinos in five southwestern states with voter registration, how to get ahead financially, and improve their communities. Armando had read in the paper that I had been promoted to a cashier of a local bank and wanted to talk to me about a job as Economic Development Director for Latinos in five southwestern states.

My initial response was, *Who is this guy?* But I agreed to meet him for lunch and it was one of the best decisions I've ever made. Armando told me about the council and I fell in love with the concept immediately. The idea of helping people in the Latino community really appealed to me. I remember how my dad used to feel when he was on the city council in Glendale, Arizona, and here was an opportunity not only based in Phoenix, but also to work in states like Arizona, Texas, Colorado, New Mexico, and California. I sensed the opportunity of being exposed and being involved could give me the education I wanted. I understood my roots. I understood what it meant to be Latino. I also knew business. My banking experience really came into play at this point.

Getting involved in the early days of what has now evolved into the National Council of La Raza was the break I'd been dreaming about. It was the late 1960s and Herman Gallegos was one of the founding members of the organization. Herman was the mentor I was looking for. He was so suave and articulate. He could speak to anyone. I thought, *Wow, I want to be like that guy someday!* I saw him in action at board meetings. I saw him in action many times with Senators and Congressional people. One time we were in a meeting with the White House. I was a fly on the wall, watching Herman deal with issues. It was like a light bulb went on and I remember thinking, *Maybe learning what he knows will help me accomplish my financial goal!*

The journey Herman and I shared was the journey of making life easier for people from the Latino community. He had a passion for that, as did I, and he taught me that you can help communities, regardless of what area you are involved in. You can do that by being a good teacher. You can do that by being a good coach. You can do that by being a good employer. You can do that by being a politician and influence policies that eventually help out many people. But perhaps the greatest lesson Herman taught me is that there are always bigger fish to catch. That philosophy is what inspired us to put together the Minority Enterprise Small Business Investment Corporation (MESBIC) doing business as La Raza Investment Company (LRIC). MESBIC allowed us to do some different things for the community in a way we hadn't done before on a much bigger scale.

We were the first organization ever funded to have a license to do business in a five-state area. I practically lived in Washington D.C. for two years to get that license approved. The knowledge and education about business I received from this was priceless. The Ford Foundation granted our organization a million dollars and we were able to leverage that million dollars 10 to 1 and do even more. All of sudden we had $11M in the bank. We could now help minorities get into business. I was the organization's first president. I was a founding father. I was able to manage MESBIC because of my experience in the bank. I learned how to be articulate and communicate with government agencies. Herman had a lot to do with that.

Herman became the Committee Chair of the Southwest Council Economic Development Committee and we got to see a lot of each other. As Director of Development, I sat down with him many times and planned strategies. Through my work with the committee, I was introduced to national organizations and governmental agencies in Washington D.C.[1] Flying back and forth between Phoenix and D.C., I learned a lot about the United States government and its agencies. Then I started going to New York regularly, meeting with the Ford Foundation people and getting the education I never would have gotten in college. In fact, my time working there was a lovely way of educating myself since I knew I would never get back to school again. And for the next six years, what an education I had!

One day I had to pick up Herman in Phoenix and take him to northern Arizona for a board retreat for the officers of the SWCLR. Herman and I really got to know each other on that car ride. We talked a lot, then stopped and got something to eat before heading on to the conference.

He said, "Lopez, are you from Glendale, Arizona?"

I said, "Yes, I am," wondering how he knew this about me.

"Is your dad Victor Lopez?" he asked.

I said, again with amazement, "Yes, he is."

He said, "I know your Uncle Vince. Do you know our story?"

I told him I didn't.

"Your Uncle Vince was wounded in the Philippines and was blinded by a grenade when he was down in a foxhole during World War II. I lost my leg during World War II in Europe. Vince and I were two of the first Latino

---

[1] The Small Business Administration (SBA), the Department of Commerce (DOC), and the Department of Housing and Urban Development (HUD)

students to be accepted at San Jose State in California. Vince couldn't see and needed eyes. I needed a job because of my leg, so the VA put us together and they paid me to be your Uncle Vince's eyes. We graduated from San Jose State, and Vince and I both went back and got our Master's degrees and now I have my Doctorate. That's why I started looking at the disparities in our Latino community, and this is why I've helped write this paper to get the Ford Foundation to fund the SWCLR."

The connection Herman had to my family only made our bond stronger.

After that, the fun really began! Herman and I were working closely together. I was interviewing and helping Latinos put together business cases, business studies, and provide equity capital. My staff and I assisted Latinos in getting bank financing. I had to travel a lot. The support I had from Pat -- who was a mom seven days a week to our children who didn't have their father around much because of my demanding work schedule -- was extraordinary. When I was home, I had to be Dad, and it was difficult for us to manage that transition. But we made it, as many people do. Now we have five, lovely, entrepreneurial children in our lives: three daughters and two sons. Another legacy!

My experience working with Herman Gallegos has helped me all my life. It's helped me understand how to approach issues and people when challenges arise, as they always do. From Herman's example, I've learned to surround myself with exceptionally well-trained people in order to get results. When I was helping people applying for loans with banks, one of the biggest pieces of advice I would tell them is to surround yourself with good people, just like Herman taught me.

I told every applicant, "You can't do this business properly unless you get yourself incorporated and get advice from an attorney. You're going to need an accountant who can tell you what running a business is really like and who can analyze your business position and help you do business the correct way, within our government, within our states, and within our cities. You need top managers who know your business and can advise you on your business so that you can get ahead at any given time. Once you work hard to make money, you've got to find a way to manage it and share some of it.

I continue to pass on that same advice today.

Twelve years ago, my Uncle Vince turned 80 and had a party in San Jose. I contacted Herman and said, "I would like you to be my guest at my

Uncle Vince's 80th birthday party." He accepted my invitation, of course, and my uncle was ecstatic.

It was during that weekend when I said to Pat, "I've got to do something someday to thank this man." Three months later, Pat and I took a trip to San Francisco, and we got together with Herman, his wife and a couple other friends to honor Herman. I wrote up some notes and talked about the successes of the Lopez family and how our business, Lopez Foods, is directly connected to Herman, the man who mentored me.

"Herman," I said, "Thank you."

Two years later, he and I were in Oakland together. We were both receiving major awards from the National Association of Latino Elected Officials (NALEO). We were sitting at the same table and as I was giving my speech, I brought the house down when I held my trophy above my head and yelled, "For me to be sharing an honor at the same time my mentor gets an award is truly remarkable! Herman, thank you!" Everyone in the place jumped to their feet and gave us a standing ovation. It was pretty cool!

I feel fortunate that I've had the chance to thank him many times over the years for the influence he's had on me as an entrepreneur. Of all the things Herman did for me over the years, one thing in particular stands out. Whenever he saw my wife Pat, he always said to her, "John is becoming very successful and very influential. But I gotta tell you, Pat. When we go out to dinner and do things for business, we always end up talking about you and your kids. That's what impressed me most about John from the very start – **family always comes first.**"

He was right. Family has always come first. Even though I've come a long way since those early days of stacking cans and sweeping floors in my parent's grocery store, I've never forgotten the lessons I learned from them. I'm grateful every day for Mom, Dad and Herman's support and belief in me. They each played a significant role in the business success Pat and I have had as McDonald's owner-operators, owners of Lopez Foods, and today, the owners of Suenos, a company in the hotel industry. Because of their influence, I am able to pass on a legacy of my own. That alone has made achieving my goal of becoming a millionaire not only worthwhile, but far better than I ever imagined living the American Dream could be. It wouldn't mean a thing if I didn't have my family to share it with. It is rewarding that our five children have become entrepreneurs. My wife and I were honored to help them get started. Another generational influence we are proud to have continued. Thankfully, I've been more than blessed with incredible children, grandchildren, and great grandchildren -- and can confidently say the Lopez legacy will live on for generations to come.

Behind the Scenes Takeaway

When I was interviewing John, I was particularly moved by how much he loved and respected his parents. Because of them, he picked up on the importance of getting your hands dirty, running a business and interacting with your customers, which was the foundation of his success! One of the biggest takeaways from his story is if you have the entrepreneurial spirit, go for it! A great mentor and role model will guide that journey and notice what truly matters to their protégé beyond the work environment. In this story, Herman recognized it was family first for my dad. Education isn't always in a classroom, after all. It can also come from the school of hard knocks and everyday experiences.

Key Question for Personal Reflection

What's one overarching goal you'd like to achieve to make your American Dream come true?

A Medical Love Story

by Dr. Robin Hall

Honoring Dr. James R. Hall

I was 13 years old when my grandmother died. Her health had been declining for a while, and she was in a coma with an inoperable brain tumor. Her prognosis wasn't good.

One night, my parents got a call from someone on staff at the nursing home where she was living. I was sound asleep when they came into my room and woke me up to tell me the news that she wouldn't make it through the night. Unlike most 13-year-old kids who would want to stay home in bed, I begged my parents to let me go with them to see my grandmother. I quickly got dressed and jumped in the back of the car.

Once we got to her room, I sat next to her bed and held her hand. A few minutes later my dad walked down the hall to get coffee. I was still holding her hand when she took her last breath. Right before she passed, I remember feeling sad, but at the same time, I was thinking about what was happening to her. Why couldn't the doctors do anything to help her? I wanted to know why. I've been inquisitive ever since I can remember, and I have a natural mind for science and problem solving. It's one of the reasons I became a doctor. My mother said that growing up, I asked "why" about everything – it didn't matter what it was; I wanted to understand what I was seeing and experiencing. I loved science and took science courses in school, but becoming a doctor was honestly not on my radar screen as a potential career. When I was growing up, I didn't know a woman could even be a doctor. Career choices for girls included becoming a nurse, teacher, or a secretary. No one was advocating that girls could be doctors, too.

At that time, there was one female doctor in the area where I lived; female physicians just weren't around. However, I knew I wanted to do something in the medical field. I was passionate about how the body works. Without any female role models to inspire me, though, I didn't have much direction. It wasn't until I was in college and working at a hospital when a couple of physicians there saw my interest in and acumen for medicine and said: "Why don't you apply to medical school?"

So at the end of college I applied, and I was put on the alternate list the first year. This upset me, but I decided to focus on the good things in my life. I graduated with a major in biology and a minor in business, and it was the smartest thing I've ever done. I went right to work in the oil business until it started failing, and then I got hired in sales management for Procter & Gamble, where I started building a successful career.

But in the back of my mind, the question nagged at me: *Should I apply to medical school again?* I was doing very well at P&G. I had a bright future there. Walking away from the money and taking out loans for medical school was a hard decision. Turns out, it would be the second smartest thing I've ever done. Had I not applied to medical school again, I never would have met my husband, Dr. James R. Hall, who has since changed my life in many ways.

I started medical school in 1984, almost four years after I was out of college. Male chauvinism was pervasive. As a female student, I was regularly subjected to stereotyping, sexual harassment, and hazing. The hours were long and regulations about limiting shifts to 12 hours weren't in place yet. Add to that a rigorous and demanding curriculum, and I wanted to quit more times than I can count.

Thankfully, I met Jim and we were married in my junior year of medical school. He provided me with more reassurance and moral support than I believed any one person ever could. He had been a medical school professor for years, and he had grown up in a medical family. His dad was a physician, his mom was a nurse, and he completely understood the pressures of going to medical school. No matter how hard things got, he encouraged me to keep going. I remember getting frustrated several times, saying I cannot go back. I'd never had to work that hard in high school or college, and the demands were pushing me to my limit.

One time, I remember being particularly upset about not doing well on one of my exams. We were sitting in the car, and he reached over and held my hand, listening intently as I talked through my inner turmoil over bombing the test. He didn't stare me down, but was present with me. He didn't try to fix my problem, or say, "You have to stay in there" or "Yeah,

I think you should quit." He simply listened and let me vent as I worked through my emotions. This would become a familiar and comfortable pattern in our marriage, one that has lasted for close to 30 years now.

"You're as smart as the next person," he said. "Don't let one test get in your way. I believe in you and support any decision you make. If you decide to stay, I'll support that decision. If you decide medical school is not the right thing, I'll support that, too." Of anything he could have said, I needed to hear those words most. He was my rock, and he was going to love me whether I got my medical degree or not. As a clinical psychologist, he knows how to ask the right questions and lead a person through challenging times. He was supportive to me then and continues to support me today.

I'll never forget when I opened my first practice, a little boy came in to see me. He was around three or four years old and for some reason, he blurted out, "Mommy, can boys be doctors, too?" I smiled to myself, thinking, *Finally! I've arrived!* When I told Jim the story, he smiled back at me with a twinkle in his eye and said, "Was there ever any question?"

Throughout my career, Jim has been there for me. When faced with limits or obstacles, my tendency has been to break through the glass ceiling, so to speak, and step outside what the majority are doing. When I've taken on projects over the years, people close to me have said things like "Are you crazy?" and "That's not gonna work!" Jim, on the other hand, always says, "If this is what you believe in, I can see you doing this and I'll support you."

Medicine is very competitive and I have a very competitive nature. I like to win and when I feel like a failure, it's tough. We don't control everything in life, and that's one of the many lessons Jim has taught me. He likes to say, "Remember, you're not perfect. Don't judge yourself based on one experience that didn't go like you wanted it to." Thankfully, he reminds me from time to time when my perfectionist tendencies come out and get the better of me.

When this happens, he'll say, "Time out. I just want you to think about this for a second." He always says this gently, with such love and caring, that I don't feel threatened or the need to get defensive. I know he has my best interests at heart.

I've been in practice for almost 25 years now and the more couples I've worked with, the more I've come to understand how special and rare the support I get from Jim truly is. He's made a lot of sacrifices for me, and he never once complained. When I decided to sell my very successful practice and take us down to one income while I plotted my next career move, our lives changed in many ways. Despite the financial and emotional stress this decision put us under, he said, "I trust your judgement." I feel very blessed that I've had someone who has reinforced my business acumen, my passion for medicine, my entrepreneurial spirit and my knowledge base. Having someone in your corner who believes in you and your mission is critical for long-term success.

Having him in my corner was especially important when I discovered the concept of concierge medicine and founded Destination Health. Destination Health is a concierge, or membership based, medical practice designed for a limited number of individuals. The difference between it and a standard medical practice has to do with the number of patients a doctor sees in a day. By taking care of fewer patients, a doctor is able to spend more time with each patient and delve more deeply into their health issues. At Destination Health, we offer comprehensive executive level physical exams and provide an evidenced based heart attack and stroke prevention program that includes an emphasis on genetics. Previously working in managed care models, I had to see patients as quickly as possible in order to be profitable. I didn't have time to talk about nutrition, or what was going on at home, or underlying issues that might be manifesting as the patient's symptoms. The model of care was basically "a pill for every ill."

When I discovered the concierge medicine model, I felt like I'd hit the jackpot because I'm able to deliver personalized medical care to all my patients. Jim could also see right from the beginning how much more rewarding this model would be for me. It aligns so well with my philosophy of getting to know my patients as individuals. I get to look at all aspects of their health, and the amazing outcomes they experience speak to the quality of the model.

But like any new venture, naysayers came out of the woodwork when I decided to open Destination Health. People who I thought would support me said things like "I can't believe you're going to do that" and "How's that going to work?" Moving forward with something new can be hard enough. When you're tired and you're around people who don't have the same values as you do, it can beat you down and you can forget who you are in the midst of it all.

Again, Jim was right there by my side, saying, "You are a beautiful, confident and smart woman. Don't let anyone discourage your dream!"

Destination Health is now ten years old and a successful and rewarding venture. I feel fulfilled knowing that I am truly saving lives and helping people age healthier.

I have also been fortunate to have been influenced by great teachers and personal development experts. My medical residency director, Dr. Henry Delisle, was stern but also saw the best in people. I found out that he complimented me on my skills to others and unknowingly helped with my self-esteem.

When I was practicing in Colleyville and becoming more and more frustrated with meeting production goals, I discovered Dr. Jayne Gardner, a life coach and psychologist. At that time, I was overcommitted in the community and in work roles. My thought process was that I needed to be involved. However, I didn't need more patients. My panel had been at capacity for some time. She encouraged me to get off all the boards I was on.

She said, "Robin, you're a lot bigger than this. You're limiting yourself." I knew she was right. Once I got rid of things that were distractions to me, bigger opportunities became clear. I give her credit for helping me recognize that I was limiting my own potential. Once the distractions were gone, Destination Health was the resulting vision.

In December this year, Jim and I will celebrate our 30th wedding anniversary. He still brings me flowers and gives me cards. He tells me he loves me several times a day. He does things that I don't always think about. For instance, I might mention without thinking much about it that I need to go get my car washed. The next thing I know, he's taken it and gotten it cleaned and put gas in it. I'm always thinking about the next thing I need to accomplish that's on my "to do" list, and he can just go with the flow.

He's also as good a listener today as he was in the early days when we sat in the car holding hands while I cried about how hard medical school was. He's learned to say when I come to him with a problem, "Do you want me to just listen or do you want advice?" He's proud of me and we share a mutual respect. He never complains when I come home late. He always waits on dinner for me, no matter how late it gets. Even when I tell him to go ahead and eat, he doesn't. I can't say enough about him. He cooks, he goes to the grocery store, he does the laundry, plus excels in his career. Most importantly, God is at the center of his life and our marriage.

Jim is a neuropsychologist and tenured professor at the University of North Texas Health Science Center/Texas College of Osteopathic Medicine. He's frequently invited to do local and international talks. When I think of him, I think of someone who is confident and comfortable in his own skin. He's humble. He is very patient and not quick to rush to any kind of judgment. He's brilliant, and he has a very high IQ that confirms my perception. His knowledge base is different than mine. Jim is a gifted researcher, having published numerous manuscripts in medical journals on dementia and other topics in his field. Jim is also quiet, so many people don't know all of his accomplishments; he's not a self-promoter. I'm very social and he's not, but he's also very fun and fun-loving, qualities I appreciate in him.

Most of all, I admire who he is and what he's accomplished. He's had dreams and aspirations and stayed with them despite obstacles along the way. He's met all the goals he's set for himself, and I am proud of him for that. I've never had to worry about having a lazy, couch potato husband. Being a good father and a good husband have been top priorities, too, and he takes all of his roles seriously.

I don't think I would be where I am today in my career if it hadn't been for Jim. My journey really is **a medical love** story. I probably would have done something different and gone a different way had I not been in his presence or had his influence in my life. I believe he was put in my life for a reason, and I was put in his for a reason, too. I couldn't be more grateful for that and look forward to the many more wonderful years we will have together.

Behind the Scenes Takeaway

When I was talking to Dr. Hall, I was so moved by how much she loves her husband. There is no question they have mutual love and respect for one another, reinforcing the universal connection between belief and support. Dr. Hall's story also emphasizes the value of listening. I recognized how important having a spouse who loves and respects you is to long-term success. Her journey to becoming a doctor is the perfect blend between doing what you love and being with the one you love. How lucky is she to have both!

Key Question for Personal Reflection

Who has been a good listener in your life?
Do you consider yourself a good listener?
Why or why not?

Three Little Words

by Bryant McKeon

Honoring Jim "Jimbo" McGhee

When we are young, we can make a lot of decisions without really understanding why we make them. It's only once we get older and take the time to reflect on the source of our decisions that we gain a deeper understanding of the meaning of our life. Some decisions are influenced by our subconscious, while others are shaped by external forces, like circumstances or people. It was cool when I understood this idea for the first time and was able to make the connection between how much my grandfather has influenced me and why I do the things I do today.

My grandfather's name is Jim "Jimbo" McGhee, and he is 77 years old. I've always called him Paw Paw, and he's been married to my Maw Maw for more than fifty years. Paw Paw has been a man of God for most of his life. He was Baptist while growing up, started his career as a Methodist preacher, then became an Episcopalian minister, and ultimately became a Catholic priest. He took his religious journey and figured out Catholicism was the right fit for him. I asked him about it once, and he said becoming Catholic was like a homecoming.

My grandfather is known for his sense of humor in his church. Paw Paw is one of the few priests there who includes jokes in his homilies. He has two sides to his personality -- his more serious side when he's delivering his weekly message, and his other side, which is more like a jokester. When we're sitting around the table and he tells a joke that he's told for the thousandth time, everyone still laughs and it's just as genuine. What makes his joke telling so precious is not necessarily the joke itself as much as his delivery and the joy he gets from telling it. He knows he's told it a thousand times. It's something he likes doing and he laughs at himself. He'll laugh before he finishes the joke!

The Ones Who Believed

When we were kids, my sister, brother and I would try to one-up each other when he told us jokes. If I got him to laugh at my joke, my sister would try to come up with a better one and make him laugh longer. We loved his jokes and his stories. Like his jokes, he loves to tell the same stories over and over again, but the one story that influenced me the most was the one about the Peace Corps. After hearing him talk about it, I looked into joining the Peace Corps but discovered it has become so popular now that a college degree is required to join.

Looking into the Peace Corps led me to learn about AmeriCorps, which is its sister organization. AmeriCorps engages adults in intensive volunteer community service work to help meet needs in various communities around the United States. The branch of AmeriCorps I got into is FEMA, which is the natural disaster relief arm. Had it not been for Paw Paw's stories and rants about how he believed nobody is really ready for college right after high school, I wouldn't be living the life I live today. He believed, most likely based on his own experience, that maturity levels out of high school are not yet up to par with what's necessary to reach your full potential and fully reap the benefits of a college education at that point in your life. He believes it's better to wait and get some life experiences under your belt. For most of my family, this side rant at the dinner table came across as something to be taken lightly, just another one of Paw Paw's outdated beliefs.

But I really believed it and took it to heart. The idea of doing something different before college was interesting to me. Not only can it change your whole outlook on college, but it can change your whole outlook on life. I'm 17, and by taking a gap year after graduating from high school this year, I've chosen to follow a path that is different than the one most of my peers are taking -- to enter college straight out of high school. But I'm okay with that. Because Paw Paw is a man who believes in the potential I could never see for myself, I trust what he says. I like to call him my "Encourager for Greatness." He doesn't say much, but when he does say something, it's elegant and powerful. He gets his point across without needing to use a lot of words.

I'll never forget the one day he said **three little words** to me that would shape the direction of my life.

I cannot recall the exact age, but it must have been around when I was 13 years old. Walking into my grandparent's house that day, I was greeted with the warm smell of my favorite snack of tomato soup and a grilled cheese sandwich, made fresh by grandmother. After indulging in the gooey, cheesy goodness, I sank into the brown leather couch next to my grandfather who was watching television. I loved that couch then, and I love it still today. You sink into it when you sit down and it feels like home.

Little House on the Prairie sang from the TV in the background as my grandfather and I crunched on our traditional bowl of popcorn. We always have a bowl of popcorn when I go to his house. For some reason, I started spouting off about how much I would enjoy being involved in film production or the entertainment industry. I went on and on about this, talking big about acting and the movies. Expecting the usual response of casual agreement before moving on to a different subject, I was caught off guard by his direct and simplistic response to my outburst.

"So do it," he said.

As I mentioned earlier, my grandfather has always been a man of few words. This time, there was something bigger behind those three. He meant it. He believed it.

So do it.

It doesn't take a million dollars and an hour-long pep talk to know someone truly believes in you. For me, those three little words were all it took. It was so simple. I said I wanted to do something and he told me to do it. There was no long, drawn-out explanation of why I should do something else first. He simply told me to go for it.

So. Do. It.

I had never heard him say these words before, and I haven't heard him say them again since. But I'll always remember that moment when he told me to do what I wanted to do. It wasn't nonchalant. He meant every word. Those three little words were exactly the right thing to say at a time in my life when I needed to hear them most.

My parents had gotten a divorce about a year before this. It was a rough time for me. Being the middle child, I took the divorce very hard and was spending a lot of my time trying to deal with the changes to my family. But that day on the couch was a click moment for me, opening my eyes and snapping me out of the trance I'd been in. I realized I didn't have to sit in a gloomy state all day worrying about what was going to happen with my parents. Instead, I could concentrate on me and my life. I could go to auditions or work on videos. He helped me shift my focus to my life. Making that shift led me to realize that success is a choice. I had potential. I had the power to make any choice I wanted. From that day forward, I adopted Paw Paw's three little words "So do it!" as my motto, and I have lived by them ever since.

I felt vulnerable admitting to Paw Paw that I want to be an actor. Obviously, acting is something a lot of people would like to do and isn't necessarily a realistic career. Hearing him encourage me made me believe I could do whatever I wanted if I put my mind to it. I felt honored to know he believes I'm capable of achieving what I say I want. He is polished and has it all together. He exudes confidence. When there's someone like that you can look at and say they are living their life exactly as they want to live it, it's an honor when they suggest you have the ability to do the same thing, too. And they respect you as an equal.

Another reason that day on the couch was so symbolic for me is what he said didn't just apply to my situation at the time of wanting to become an actor. His words applied to *everything*. They were universal. There are no tricks or secrets to getting what you want in life. You just have to do what it takes to get what you want. If there was ever a phrase I needed to hear, that was the one. I don't like the idea of saying, "This is my dream" and then not accomplishing that dream. I'm going to do what it takes.

My generation -- the Millennials -- knows we can have everything right now. That doesn't mean we want everything right now. The way things are set up in the world today makes us feel entitled. We've been programmed for entitlement. The world Paw Paw grew up in was very different. He had a rough childhood. Both of his parents were deaf, and he had to learn sign language to communicate with them. The kind of technology we have today and take for granted just wasn't available back then. When he was almost 16 years old, both his parents died, and he had to figure out a lot of things on his own. I will never fully grasp the bravery and valor he possesses, but from what I have seen, I hope that by realizing the impact he's had on my life, he can see the good he has done.

My hopes would be for him to realize, perhaps through my gratitude, the influence he's had on so many people. I hope that one day, I can give back what he's given to me. I have never formally thanked my grandfather, but I intend to do that very soon. Our relationship has always been a soft-spoken one, but I owe it to him to give gratitude where it is due. I'm getting ready to go away for ten months and that scares me. It's time I let him know how much I appreciate what he's done for me. That is the greatest way to honor him.

    We never know how what we say or do will come back to us. **By being genuine, honest and real -- that's when impact is made.** When we are really listening to someone, we are able to take action on what they say, not just hear their words. Living in the present and really listening can go a long way. If I had to bottom line the significance my grandfather has had in my life, I would say he saved me when he spoke those three little words. They moved me out of my depression and into an awareness inside myself where I could make conscious decisions about what I want to do with my life. His advice was the key that opened the door to my happiness. I still have to unlock that door and choose to step through it, but what matters is that it's there now. I can see it. And no one can take that away from me.

Behind the Scenes Takeaway

When I was interviewing Bryant, I was struck by his conviction about knowing you can move your life forward, especially after unexpected circumstances. The relationship between a grandparent and a grandchild is a unique dynamic brimming with opportunity for guidance and mentorship. One of the biggest takeaways from his story is how powerful it is when we have a real conversation with someone we respect who is truly present and listens to what we say.

Key Question for Personal Reflection

What is your motto?
What words do you live your life by?

Editor's Note: Pastor Jim McGhee (aka Paw Paw) was laid to rest on April 23, 2016. Before he passed, Bryant was able to read to him this story in the hospital and express his love, gratitude and appreciation.

Behind Closed Doors

by Nicole Gibson

Honoring Sherry Kelly

I love sunny days. They make me happy. I especially love sunny days when the leaves move on the trees in a light breeze. Days like these symbolize hope and new beginnings, reminding me of what's good in the world. They also take me back to the moment when I realized I loved my mom more than ever and could forgive her for becoming addicted to drugs during the tender years of my early adolescence.

My mom's name was Sherry Darlene Demus-Kelly. She was a very special person because she could make anyone feel good about life. She loved to go out and see people as often as she could. One of the things she enjoyed was taking my older sister and me in her car and driving through my grandmother's neighborhood. As a nine-year-old in the back of the car, I knew what we were going to do and where we were going. I knew what street we were going to drive down. Honestly, I didn't like those car rides. I didn't want to go on them, but they really grew on me. I didn't appreciate the detours and side stops and visits with people in the neighborhood until four or five years later when we stopped doing them altogether.

Mom took me and my sister out almost every weekend. Saturday mornings started the same way every week. My older sister and I got up and took a bath. Then Mom combed our hair and got us into our clothes. When we drove down my grandmother's street, we stopped at every other house where Mom would visit with the neighbors. It didn't matter what their status in life was; Mom stopped and talked to them. There wasn't a person she didn't know. Everyone was always so happy to see her. She made everyone feel like they mattered, and she was always, always smiling. I'm not like that, but she made me want to be that way. Even to this day, I find myself asking, "What would Mom do in this situation?" Despite her struggles with addiction, she was that big of an influence on me. In the end, she never knew how she positively impacted my life through this very painful period.

As a child, though, I didn't understand anything beyond my own despair over eventually losing her to drugs.

I was in 5th grade when my mom became addicted to crack cocaine. She was a functioning drug addict who worked as a professional cook during the day and smoked drugs at night. She was able to provide for me and my sister very well. But once drugs entered the picture, our lives literally changed overnight. Mom's love for cooking in the kitchen became a tradition for our family. We went from my mom cooking dinner every night to my older sister cooking for us and Mom being in the background. Her addiction changed my relationship with her, and I was mad at her for a long time.

I remember the very last time my sister and I helped Mom cook. We were having green bean casserole. I hated green bean casserole, but I loved being in the kitchen with Mom.

I was slicing cheese and chopping onions. My sister said, "Make sure you slice the cheese diagonally."

I didn't know what diagonally meant. I didn't think it mattered, so I sliced it in squares.

My sister said, "That's not right." She took the corners of the cheese and cut them off. I was upset about this but, little did I know, cutting cheese into diagonal shapes would be the least of my worries moving forward.

The next time we were supposed to cook was for Christmas. And we didn't. The next time we were supposed to cook after that was for New Year's. And again, we didn't. I could tell things were different, but I wasn't old enough yet to recognize the signs of addiction or understand what was happening.

The new year came. One Saturday morning, I needed my shirt ironed. My mom was taking my sister and me out, and being dressed properly was one of her rules. Without thinking about anything other than the task at hand, I burst into her room and discovered her doing drugs.

I said, "Mom, what are you doing?" I had never been exposed to drugs before and didn't know what I was seeing.

I can remember the look of panic and shame in her eyes when she realized what I saw. She said quickly, "Everything's okay! I'll iron your shirt!" before rushing me out of her room.

It wasn't long after this before everything that was special to me stopped. The cooking. The car rides to grandma's neighborhood. Mom's attention. I was mad because there was no explanation. So I thought, *Let me do what's important to her. Let me focus on school.* Mom said I had to come home and do my homework first before anything else. That was always important to her. In my young mind I thought maybe she would be more attentive if I was doing what mattered to her. I thought maybe our life would go back to the way it was if I did well in school. I blamed myself for why the things that mattered so much stopped. I knew she was different, but I still didn't know why.

But being a good student didn't change anything. In fact, things went from bad to worse. We eventually had to move out of our house and move in with my grandma. Everything was a blur. I didn't understand why we had to move. No one ever explained why she stopped cooking or taking us on car rides. Even though I didn't like them at the time, when I didn't have them anymore, I really wanted those car rides back.

I was mad about everything. And I stopped talking to just about everyone.

My mom struggled with her emotions, and she struggled with my grandma. Both of these struggles played into her addiction. Up until the time she was 28 years old, my mom gave half her paycheck to my grandmother. Years later when I asked her why she did that, Mom said she wanted to feel like her mother loved her. Before my mother passed, they were able to speak openly about their relationship, and my grandmother told my mom that she *did* love her.

"I just show love in a different way," Grandma said.

Living with her mom again as an adult didn't work out for long. My mom was a free spirit, and Grandma wanted her back at the house at a certain time. She wasn't having any of that, so she moved us to my cousins' house. They lived in a nice home across from a golf course. They had new clothes, new shoes and video games. One of the things they didn't have, though, was real food.

Their mom came home in the morning and went back out again at night for her job. The children were left on their own to take care of themselves. They had things like cereal and juice, and they were always eating junk. I was raised on home cooking. Their food situation was foreign and strange to me.

My cousins were mean to me and my sister. They didn't want us to touch any of their things. Mom would soften the situation for us, saying,

"Don't worry about it. They're just being kids. It's not you. They probably don't want you in their space."

But their rude comments and stinginess still made us feel bad. I resented them because they mistreated us, and I spent a lot of energy being angry. Everything I'd ever known was different. Once I found out what drugs were and that Mom was addicted, I became even more angry than I'd been. I lashed out at people and wasn't a nice daughter anymore. Once her addiction started, I'd been acting like the adult in the family and I'd had enough. Mom would ask me to do things, and I'd politely tell her *no*. I didn't yell and I wasn't rude, but I said *no*. She got mad at me every time and said, "What is your problem?" I eventually did what she asked.

Looking back, I wish I would have been nicer. I just didn't know how. I was caught up in a storm of anger, teenage hormones and confusion about what was happening. And through all this, Mom continued to be nice to people everywhere she went.

I eventually realized that my cousins' mom was also on drugs. I found out after noticing that she and my mom went into the bathroom together and locked the door every day around the same time. I wasn't trying to be a detective. I just wanted to know why we were living at my cousins' house!

Although anger can make you feel powerful, being angry all the time is exhausting and boring. Subconsciously, I knew I couldn't be mad at Mom forever. But I was stubborn and hurt, so I kept up my defenses and spent a lot of my time silently fuming.

Then something happened one Friday night that snapped me out of my misery and opened my eyes to the power of forgiveness.

My sister and I were dressed and waiting for Mom in her car. It was our night to go out to dinner as a family, a tiny bright spot in an otherwise dark time for me. Mom came outside shortly after my sister and I got into the car and asked us what we were doing.

"Waiting for you!" we said.

"Get back in the house and get your cousins!" she said.

I couldn't believe what she was saying. Didn't she know how badly they treated us? Didn't she know I wanted nothing to do with them? I did not want to get them, but she made me!

Once they found out they were going out to eat with us, they became super excited. They got into the car and Mom started to drive. In that moment, I stared at her, boiling inside. How could she be so nice to them when they were nothing but rude to us?

Then it dawned on me. My mom was as nice as she was to my mean cousins because she understood that *everyone* in that car was going through something. We were essentially all the same, yet different. She was struggling with addiction. My cousins were hungry and malnourished. I was angry at the world for dealing me a rotten hand. If she knew I'd had an epiphany, she never showed any sign she knew because she kept talking and driving while I kept staring, trying to wrap my head around this new-found insight. If she could forgive them for mistreating us, I could forgive her. I had to.

From that point on, I saw my mom differently. I loved her more than I ever had in my life. Later she said things like, "You're so nice to me. Why are you being so nice to me?" I just hugged her harder and kissed her more. It was the least I could do, given the circumstances. I'd lost enough years of my young life. I didn't want to lose any more.

To an outsider, that moment may seem small and insignificant. It was an ordinary day, after all. A Friday night like any other Friday night with a family going out to dinner. But for me, that moment changed my life forever. That was the day I understood the universal truth that everyone has more going on than what they show to the world. It could be addiction. It could be depression. It could be going without food. It's easy to believe other people have things so great, when the truth is, they may be silently suffering **behind closed doors** while putting on their best smile.

A wave of emotion came over me that day. It's hard to describe or explain, but something changed in me forever. I believe that experience contributed to why, today, I have the attitude that there's always a way out. There's always a way to fix a problem. I choose to be positive about life, which can be off-putting to some people. In fact, people have told me over the years, "Nicole, everything isn't always positive!" My life wasn't positive for those few years in my teens. But in that moment when my mom was positive to my cousins and showed them grace, I realized things weren't that bad, and I could be a bigger person, too.

I'm more understanding and compassionate today as a result of that experience. I'm not easily offended. If someone says something negative or rude, I don't take it personally. I recognize they're lashing out because something's going on in *their* life, not because of me.

Mom's lessons definitely influence me in my professional life. At work, I've been told my management style is fair. My team feels safe about coming to me with questions or challenges. They trust me, and I'm proud I've created a work environment where my team can do this. I know who

I am and what I stand for. I'm comfortable with that, and it shows in the way my team functions.

When someone is in front of us, we never know what their real story is. I work at an airport and see many different types of people every day. I wonder about them. Are they in love? Do they have children? Did they wake up this morning in a good mood or bad mood? How did they grow up? Did they run through the fields as kids? You just never know what's going on behind the closed doors of people's lives. In my 37 years, I've come to understand that everyone is going through something. And no matter how bad their lives may be, there's always room in our hearts to forgive others. Mom showed me that, and I will always be grateful she did.

Toward the end of her life, Mom got sick and had to stop doing drugs. In those last ten years, we were able to talk openly about the past. I distinctly remember our conversation when I told her she was a great mom.

She gasped and said, "Really? You really think that?"

"Yes, Mom, I do," I said.

I don't think she ever fully recognized how great a mom she was. I'm not sure if she ever forgave herself for the time when she was doing drugs. I'm not wired like my mom, but I make an effort to be like her as a tribute to the gifts she gave to me and the world. I find myself asking, "What would Mom do?" when faced with unpleasant situations. I think this is one of the reasons people call me an old soul. In high school, I was friends with everyone. In college, I stood up for a timid Spanish professor whom other students picked on. I paid attention to his lessons and respected him. I have a deep level of empathy for others most of the time, and I have my mom to thank for that.

I think I would have been a different person today had it not been for that night in the car with my mom and my cousins. I think I would still be angry. But life is so much better when you can look at things the way my mom did: with kindness and respect for everyone, no matter their circumstances. By the time Mom died, I'd had the chance to come to terms with all that happened. She continues to shape me today in so many ways. She would always say, "Don't live your life in fear of people or things or what someone can do to you." It took a while for me to not live my life in fear, but I've reached a point where I'm less afraid and more accepting. I work hard every day on improving myself so I can be a better person. I think she'd be proud of me for that.

Behind the Scenes Takeaway

Nicole is a dear friend and as I interviewed her, I fell in love with her heart. I have known Nicole for over 20 years and I never knew about her personal hardship, which is why Behind Closed Doors is such a fitting title. The love, patience, and understanding she has for her mom and her child self is powerful. Her story really moved me when she hugged me over and over and over again, thanking me for honoring her mom. I've had the pleasure of working with Nicole and I've seen the respect she's earned from her coworkers, possibly due to her sensitivity to what people are going through as well as her outlook about there's always another way. Although this story honors Nicole's mother, it's ultimately about how Nicole had to believe in herself.

Key Question for Personal Reflection

Think about someone in your life who could be going through something difficult "behind closed doors." How could you reach out to them and brighten their day?

Success Has Many Parents

by Jim Estrada

Honoring Raymond and Julia Estrada

Becoming successful in life does not happen in isolation. I often say, "*Success has many parents, but failure is an orphan.*" To achieve great things, we must remain open to influences and learn from people who come into our lives. Although several people throughout my life helped shape me into the man I am today, my parents were my first mentors and definitely the most influential.

The kind of family you come from plays a big role in your success as an adult. Because of my upbringing, I've experienced many of life's greatest opportunities: running several of my own businesses; raising two, capable sons and watching them become adults; meeting presidents of the United States; and getting to know some of the world's most famous celebrities. I grew up in a protected environment filled with a lot of love and admiration for one another. My parents, Raymond and Julia Estrada, gave me a solid foundation for living a successful life, grounded in traditional morals and values. Who I am today and the professional success I've had can be directly traced back to those formative years of my childhood. Because of my parents, I developed a strong work ethic, learned how to earn my own way, and cultivated a sense of fairness that has served me well.

Even though my parents didn't have traditional, formal educations, they were both wise. My mom only got as far as the eighth grade, but that was a heck of an accomplishment for a Mexican- American female in the early 1930s. My dad only went as far as the fifth grade and rode a horse back and forth to school in southeastern Colorado. A lot of our extended family members and friends never understood why we had so much pride and confidence in ourselves, given our economic circumstances. After all, they had more money, better houses and better clothes than us, but we were a "tribe" (six brothers and one sister) and we believed in ourselves.

When we showed up anywhere in a car with all seven of us—plus mom and dad—we looked like canned sardines as we piled out. But we did it with such pride and had no shame about our large family.

As a couple, my parents were sociable and were very popular. When I was a kid, they had a hog ranch in Torrance, California, where they hosted a lot of parties. It was on that ranch where I saw my parents at their best. Watching them socialize was such a treat because of the way they interacted with people so naturally and smoothly; they were very much liked and could have been successful politicians. They were also jokesters with quick wits. My mom had a dry wit, and my dad was very demonstrative with his humor. My dad was like Will Rogers; to him a stranger was "just a friend he hadn't met yet." Everyone who came to our homes in Los Angeles and San Diego knew if they stopped at Raymond and Julia's, they'd be welcome, they'd be fed, they'd have drinks, and they'd have music. *Mi casa es su casa* was more than an adage; it was the core of their worlds. They taught my siblings and me that attitude and I've never forgotten it.

My parents' pride in their family and having an open, welcoming home was based on their life experiences. They believed in the value of getting both a formal and practical education. Mom taught my siblings and me how to wash, cook, iron, and clean the house. As soon as Dad came home from work, he took us all outside and taught us how to drive nails, how to build additions to the house, and just about everything you'd want to know about carpentry, masonry, cement finishing, plumbing, and electrical systems. He even taught us how to maintain and repair cars.

Our father was a philosopher at heart and liked to pass on his wisdom to his kids. He would tell my sister in Spanish, *"Hasta la valer,"* which means value yourself so you don't need to get admiration and validation from other people. If you believe in yourself, he counseled, it will become contagious. Zig Ziglar and other self-help leaders talk about the value of understanding who you are and liking who you are so that other people will naturally be attracted to you. Dad modeled this mindset in everything he did and made sure his kids understood it.

My mom passed on her wisdom through her love and belief in her children. She referred to all the boys in our family as *"mi rey"* (my king). We each had our own unique gifts and talents, and she recognized them all. No matter what we did, she always managed to spread out her praise and recognition equitably. I grew up knowing that I was smart; the wisdom she passed on to me was not to lord it over my siblings, or anyone else.

Mom taught us practical skills, too, but she pushed me academically. She emphasized the need to pay attention in school and to get good grades. Together, they were a great combination. Had she not drilled those messages into my head over and over again, I don't think I would have developed what it takes to become a self-made man.

Like many adolescent boys, when I was in my teens, the least thing I wanted to be like was my dad. He was a wonderful man, worked very hard, loved by everybody he met, but at that time of my life, I still had a lot of years ahead of me before I'd recognize how being like him was a really great thing. My mind was centered around how I was different than he was. I thought, "Hey, I'm getting an education; I'm not at all like my father."

But the truth is, I wasn't taking my school education seriously. In fact, I was bored to death. Thank goodness for Mr. Bill Bowen. He was my guidance counselor in junior high school and set the stage for success in the next phase of my life. He frequently told me, "You can do anything you want to do, Jim. You have the intelligence; you have the work ethic; you have the ability. But you have to want it." Intellectually his words made a lot of sense, but coming from a limited level of exposure in terms of what opportunities existed beyond my home life, it was as if he was talking in a foreign language to me.

Up until that time in junior high school, all I saw around me were working class people. I didn't understand what it meant to really want something. I come from a family of migrant workers. By the time I was 13, I was still helping my family pick plums and pack vegetables and grapes during our summer. I didn't relate to my teachers; I knew some of them were good and some were bad. Mr. Bowen saw something in me and took me aside, pumping me up psychologically as well as emotionally and academically, the way a great mentor does. He believed in me in a way my parents did, and that belief added another layer to the foundation of my future success.

Still, school just didn't do it for me. In spite of my innate intelligence, I wasn't tracked for college. I was tracked for vocational education. In high school I was in the vocational classes where I spent half days at the local city college for classes in auto repair, carpentry, and the like. The other half of my day I took academic classes including choir, physical education and home economics. At my high school, when I got ahead of everybody and I was being a pain in the butt to my teachers, school administrators offered me an opportunity to be an office monitor, which kept me from getting into further trouble. Thankfully, Mr. Bowen made me his office monitor.

One day, after I was caught up with my assigned filing tasks, I pulled my files from the cabinet and looked at them. I discovered my IQ at that time was 137. The gifted program started at 135. Okay, I thought, why the heck am I going to vocational school if I have an IQ of 137?

That discovery set in motion a series of events that—looking back at them today through the lens of what I now know—might not have been the most advantageous thing for a smart kid like me to do. But we all walk our own paths, and thankfully my decision to quit high school in January of my senior year didn't turn into a dead-end for me.

It was 1961, and after walking away from high school, I went straight to the military recruiting offices and asked if I could join. They said yes, but I'd have to take some tests. I scored high in the four categories they tested for and was invited to enlist and continue my education in their programs.

The Air Force recruiter said, "We'll send you to one of the best electronic schools the Armed Forces offer and make you someone who can fix most of the military equipment we use."

"What will that entail?" I asked.

He said, "Our school is 52 weeks."

I added quickly, "That's a full year!"

The news did not excite me. I thought, "Doesn't he realize I just quit school because I was bored to death? And now he's telling me I've got to go back to school for another year?"

Coming from a working-class background, I didn't have role models in our extended family of anyone who attended college or had even been in an academic environment. I knew I could make a lot of money as a carpenter because that's what my brothers and my dad were doing. But electronics sounded good—like a trendy career. With Mr. Bowen reinforcing the fact that I was bright, intelligent and able, I thought, *"What the heck. Why not?"*

So I selected the Air Force. I took classes in electronic logic and theory: how a vacuum tube works; how a transistor works; how resistance affects the operation; and a basic concept of electronics, theoretical and practical. Half the kids in the electronics school were from California and the other half were from Michigan—all had some form of college education. I was the only non-white individual in that whole class. I had to compete with kids who'd been to college and, at graduation, I came out in the top 10 percent of my class!

That was an epiphany. *"Wow,"* I thought to myself, *"Here I am, a young Chicano who didn't have a lot of exposure to mainstream society and I'm competing with guys who have a better education, and I'm among the top 10%."*

Turned out, the top 10% of the graduating class had their choice of becoming an instructor or selecting what duty stations or bases to be assigned, anywhere around the world. I decided to become an instructor. Regardless of the number of stripes on your shoulders or sleeves, the highest-ranking person in the classroom was the instructor. I thought telling other people what to do sounded pretty cool.

Even though I didn't have a lot of rank, I had accomplished things that, in my mind, were amazing. I started to think I really was somebody, regardless of the track I'd been put on in high school, pegged for manual labor and nothing more. A couple of years later, I got married in Illinois. But I missed my family and eventually returned home to California to work with my brothers, again as a carpenter.

Being back with my family was wonderful, but I quickly discovered carpentry was not what I wanted to do for the rest of my life. I remember that day so vividly. I was working with my brothers and my dad, and it was one of those hot, arid days in San Diego. The sun was beating down. I was tired and sweating and I thought, *"I don't have to do this! This is tough, and this is rough, and I really don't like it."*

So I took off my carpenter's pouch with the hammers and the nails in it, threw them down on the ground and told my dad and my older brother, "Guys, I'm through with this. See ya."

"What are you doing?" they asked, looking at me like I was crazy.

"I'm quitting!" I said.

"But you don't have a job," said my father.

"I'll figure something out," I said.

And I did. The next day I took a job working for the telephone company.

From there, I started climbing my own ladder. I enrolled at Mesa Community Junior College using the G.I. Bill and made the Dean's list during my first semester. By the end of my second year, I decided to transfer to San Diego State University and major in broadcast journalism. Through the connections of one of my journalism professors, I landed an internship in radio and television at a local station and was hired to be a television news reporter during my senior year in college. My career expanded and grew.

I was subsequently hired by the Council of Governments as the Director of Communications for the 13 cities, the County of San Diego and the state of California planning entity. I then joined the newly created Metropolitan Transit Development Board as its Communication Director and promoted the construction of the county's light rail transit system.

I was recruited to take a Marketing Supervisor position with McDonald's. Then Anheuser Busch recruited me to start their corporate giving programs in the southwest in Houston, Texas. I was soon promoted to oversee the company's Hispanic Consumer Department in St. Louis, Missouri.

Eventually I went out on my own and founded a creative PR & Marketing agency. Each time I took a new position, it was like I was going back to school, only better because I had the maturity to appreciate what I was learning and welcomed the experience with open arms.

As I became more successful as a professional, I made sure my parents knew how grateful I was for all they'd done for me. Acknowledging them, taking time with them, making sure that whenever I was able to schedule an event or an activity to celebrate family, I'd do it. When I was living in my first major house in Houston, Texas, I sent them airline tickets to come spend time with me. For Mother's Day, my siblings and I took Mom to The Westgate, the top hotel restaurant in San Diego at the time. Reinvesting back into them was my way of saying thanks. Sharing material things with them was another way I showed them how much I appreciated them.

The Cuban political philosopher and activist José Marti wrote there are three ways to ensure you leave a positive legacy in this world. First, plant a tree. Secondly, have a child. Thirdly, write a book. These three things will ensure your legacy. I've planted trees; I've picked the fruits from those trees. I have two sons and I've written a book. Everything is falling into place, and I'm in a place today where I can pass on the blessings I've received in my life.

One of the clues about corporate success I talk to audiences about today is how important it is to have mentors in your life if you want to succeed. I stress how critical it is to have someone who is going to take an interest in you and provide you with opportunities to climb the ladder to the various stages along the way. I tell them about my parents and how mentorship might start in the home like it did for me. And that it's okay, too, if it doesn't.

I also emphasize that the mentorship process is something you must reinvest in others when you've benefitted from the process. Paying it forward, especially to people who are younger than you and coming up in the world, provides huge dividends to all involved. Supporting someone who you think is going to be successful is a wise investment of your time and effort because it's going to come back to you. When you tie your rope to an ascending star, it reflects well on you. We all need successful people to help us become successful! If anything else, working with successful mentors helps us become successful faster.

The ability to mentor isn't something we're born with, though. In fact, until you become very successful and comfortable with your success, you can't become a great mentor. It's only once this threshold has been crossed that you become comfortable in a mentorship role. Mom and Dad knew this instinctively, and I can honestly say I've been blessed because of what they taught me. I've gotten more breaks in life than I probably deserve. I learned to take advantage of those breaks and grow my personal skillsets to where I am today. I'm in my senior years, and this is the best I've felt psychologically, emotionally, and physically in my entire life. Life keeps getting better!

Mom and Dad are both gone now, but their legacy lives on through their children, grandchildren, and great-grandchildren. If I could see them again today, the first thing I would say is, "I love you." Then I would say, "Thanks for watching over me from up above. I hope I've lived up to your expectations."

It's a cliché, but my life's success goes back to the strength of my family. We had each other's backs. We supported each other. It made a big difference then—and continues to make a big difference now.

Behind the Scenes Takeaway

I have two major takeaways from Jim's story. First, I agree with Raymond and Julia's perspective on the importance of a formal and practical education. Each prepares us for the real world in its own, significant way. When I was interviewing Jim, I immediately felt the passion he has for his parents and the loving foundation they instilled in him and passed on as a true living legacy. "Mi Casa Es Su Casa" is a perfect representation of his parent's Hispanic heritage for welcoming family and friends to their home and sharing their traditions with everyone. Second, I believe mentoring is a personal decision that should be passed on when the time is best for maximum impact. Reinvesting the rewards we've received from the mentorship process can be one of the most gratifying experiences of our lives.

Key Question for Personal Reflection

What will be your legacy?

The Power of Impact

by Newy Scruggs

Honoring Educators and Role Models

Throughout my life, I've had a keen awareness of influential people around me who were dedicated to making an impact in the world. I was naturally attracted to them, and I was open to receiving their guidance and wisdom. My awareness started with my parents, Albert and Theresa Scruggs, who have the greatest work ethic of any two people I have ever known. As I got older, my awareness expanded outside the home with experiences I had through church, school and work. Each experience and encounter with the ones who believed in me taught me the importance of being my own self, a lesson I work hard to pass on to others today through my career, family, and philanthropic activities.

My dad was drafted into the Army and made a career of military life. He wanted to provide the best support for me, my mom, and my sister. My mom supported our family in other ways. For one, she was around for me and my sister. She made sure our beds were made, our clothes were clean, and everything we did was done well. I first learned about being self-sufficient from her. She never told me not to do what I wanted to do, and I've had no bigger cheerleader keeping my dream alive for me than my mom. To this day, my parents are great people who believe in what I do.

From a young age, I wanted to forge my own path in the world. By the time I was 11 years old, my goal was to become a sportscaster. Despite my dad's positive experience in the military, I decided early on that a career in the armed forces wasn't a good fit for me. I knew God had put me on this earth for broadcasting. Luckily, my 5th grade teacher, E. Larry McDuffie, had experience on the radio. Outside of teaching at my elementary school, he also led the Savannah Community Choir at my church in Georgia and was a Disc-Jockey for a local R&B station on Sunday mornings and afternoons.

When I learned about his radio experience, I wasn't shy about telling him, "Man, I want to be on the radio! I want to be on the news! I want to be on TV! I want to do what you do!" Letting him know my interests got his attention. In Mr. McDuffie's class, we were required to do a mock newscast. He wanted us to learn about current events and that was a test to see if we were reading the local paper and keeping up with things. It's interesting that an assignment most of my classmates dreaded became something I loved and helped me discover my passion.

I felt on top of the world after going into the studio with Mr. McDuffie, participating in a mock newscast, and seeing the TVs on set. I was hooked immediately. It's been said that if you find something you really want to do, you will never work a day in your life. I knew at that point in my young life I had found the Holy Grail of my future career. Broadcasting was it!

Everything I did after that had something to do with sports. I played football in high school and had the chance to meet a gentleman named Tom Suiter, the main sports anchor at WRAL TV Channel 5 in Raleigh, North Carolina. I heard him speak when I visited Terry Sanford High School, and it was so exciting having the chance to ask him questions about his profession. I watched him all the time on TV. He would eventually become one of my career mentors, helping me figure out what going into television would look like for me, as well as where to go to college.

Always positive, Tom Suiter was terrific. He wrote me letters and was passionate and full of enthusiasm about the future. He introduced me to the importance of asking the question we all need to ask ourselves: *Why am I doing what I'm doing?* I didn't fully understand nor appreciate the power of this question until later in my life, but Tommy got me started asking the right questions and developing a conviction about myself and what mattered most to me. He showed me I needed to work hard, and that things are not going to be given to me.

With Dad in the military, we moved often and had been in the Fayetteville/Fort Bragg area of North Carolina from my 6th grade year until I graduated high school. I wasn't a big fan of the place. I wanted to live in Chicago like my grandfather where movie theaters played up to 18 movies at one time. There wasn't anything close to that in Fayetteville. Chicago had the Bears, Chicago had the Bulls, and all I could think was, *Wow! What would it be like to have a pro team in my town?* At that time, North Carolina was still a few years away from getting its first professional team when the Charlotte Hornets showed up in 1988.

Adolescence is a tough time for most kids, and I was no exception. Trying to figure out who you are, what you want to be, and how you want to act makes high school challenging. It's hard to decide what's right for you and too easy to blow with the wind, sometimes landing in a field with the wrong people around you. Peer pressure is fierce, and for a while, it took me off course, sidelining my forward progress and childhood dream.

I remember one time after football practice in the locker room, I was listening to music on my SONY Walkman. My friends and I liked to ask each other what we were listening to and exchange mixtapes. One day my friend pressed me to listen to my tape, but I didn't want to share it with him.

But he persisted and after grabbing my headphones and listening for a few seconds, he gave them back to me and shook his head in disbelief. I liked Sting and groups like Chicago, but from his point of view, I was "supposed" to be listening to groups like Run DMC, Public Enemy, and Big Daddy Kane. I wasn't against rap. I simply liked all types of music (except country) and wanted to listen to whatever I wanted. It was hard when my friends put me down for not being like them. Later, this music became wildly popular across the board. I must have been ahead of my time.

My success didn't come easily, though. I had challenges along the way trying to figure out what success was to me. Had it not been for my English teacher, Mr. Charles Stanton, I may have fallen prey to peer pressure and never known the blessings I now enjoy. Today, I'm married to my beautiful wife, have a career I love, and live an abundant life with my family.

Mr. Stanton was great. I didn't keep much from high school, but I did keep the brown, weathered binder from my English class. Not that I was ever in love with English, but Mr. Stanton taught it so well, it was impossible not to be impacted.

Two things in particular stood out from his class; the writings of Henry David Thoreau and Ralph Waldo Emerson crystallized for me the idea that I could be my own self. I didn't have to follow everything other people were doing. One thing Ralph Waldo Emerson talked about specifically was what genius means. He said the definition of genius is believing in one's own self. He also wrote about the rule of greatness, which states, "What I must do is all that concerns me, not what the people think." Emerson also said, "To be great is to be misunderstood."

Both writers also talked about being a nonconformist. Mr. Stanton helped me see that three things happen when you conform to what you don't believe in. One, it scatters your force. Two, it loses you time. And three, it blurs the impression of your character, which is hazy when you are 17 years old. But I took what he was teaching to heart, and I began applying what I learned in class to my life.

The combination of what I learned from Mr. Stanton and working with Tom Suiter ultimately helped me gain a laser focus of what I wanted for my life. I became focused on what I wanted to be and began to form my own truth.

Their influence led me to a book by Pat Riley called *Showtime: Inside the Lakers Breakthrough Season*. That book is about the 1987 Los Angeles Laker team. Chapter 13 is called "Motivation," and I have remembered the lessons of that chapter all these years. That book helped me earn a scholarship because it inspired me to keep my grades up and my motivation high.

One of the main ideas in Chapter 13 is that the ones who can separate themselves from the pack are those who understand what it takes to sustain excellence. To get away from a "to have" mentality. To have is something we get early in life. To have power, to have a little bit of prestige, to have position, to have the house and the car and all those things we feel we need. Then you understand later on in your career that those things don't mean anything. That when you experience them, you realize the only thing left is to be the very best.

You learn to prioritize the "to be" ahead of the "to have." You're thinking about being the very best. You're thinking about making sure that you are being a person you can be proud of. Once you believe that you want to be the best, you realize that all those other things you worried about for years, such as the money, prestige, and power, follow you wherever you go.

Instead of chasing your tail, you realize your tail follows you. At the end of that chapter, Coach Riley says, "I've been playing this game for 30 years. It's a kid's game I love, and I get paid for taking part. All of us make enormous amounts of money to go out and do something we need to do, earn a living. It's something we want to do, and when you can put those two things together, what you need and what you want, there's your motivation. Keep that situation alive. Be so good at it, they can't even think about replacing you."

In 2006 when the Miami Heat beat the Dallas Mavericks in the NBA Final, I covered that series and slipped Pat Riley a note. I said, "I want to thank you for what you wrote. It helped me get a college scholarship, and

I'm working today doing what I want to do. So much of who I am and what I'm doing today was based off your book, *Showtime*."

As I've built a successful life for myself and my family in broadcasting, I've tried to make sure that those folks who helped me along the way know what they did for me. A couple of years ago, I did a commencement speech for my alma mater, the University of North Carolina at Pembroke. While I was there, I looked for one particular math professor I'd had. When I found him in the audience, I said, "Stand up! I want to thank you. I didn't really earn that C in your class, but you saw I was trying and I appreciate it."

When a former classmate heard something good happened to me earlier this year, he congratulated me. I sent him back a note saying, "Not without you, E. Not without you." In 1992, he helped jumpstart my career when he got me a job at the CBS affiliate in Florence, South Carolina. I was shooting high school football highlights at the time, and through his connection at the station, I landed a full-time job. I've since moved on, but he still works at that TV station today. I've never forgotten his act of kindness.

I'm not sure how much Mr. Stanton was aware of how he influenced me, but my dad ended up teaching with him. He kept up with me through my dad. Dad told him how grateful I was for what I had learned in his class. Mr. Stanton passed away a few years ago. I can only hope he had a sense of how powerful his teaching was, not just for me, but for all the students who were fortunate enough to have him as their teacher.

And that really is the truth of how anyone succeeds in this life: with the help, encouragement and belief that comes from people who care enough to make a difference. I've been fortunate. I've had several people who took an interest in me and allowed me to experience **the power of impact** first-hand. As a way of giving back and paying it forward, I've set up scholarships making people aware of the opportunities in sports journalism and sports communications who might not otherwise know about their options. When I was going through school, role models didn't exist in the sports broadcasting field, paving the way for people like me. I was inspired to create my scholarship by a sports agent named Leigh Steinberg who represented several of the NFL's greatest quarterbacks including Troy Aikman and Steve Young. The movie *Jerry McGuire* is based on his story.

The Newy Scruggs Scholarship is at UNC-Pembroke and The Newy Scruggs Scholarship for Enrichment Opportunities is at the University of Texas at Arlington. Wanting to work in this field isn't some crazy pipe dream, but a viable career path. Every year I receive letters from the students who win. Reading their words is an incredible reward for me. I remember how I felt when I won my scholarships. I was so proud and read the award letters to my mom. Knowing I play a part in giving the next generation of sports journalists that same experience fills me with pride and joy.

By the time they arrived in my life, each of my believers had achieved success in theirs. Sharing with me their knowledge, explaining things to me, or simply giving me great advice shaped me into the man I am today. The magical combination of my parents, E. Larry McDuffie, Tom Suiter, Mr. Stanton, and Pat Riley's book gave me what I needed to make good decisions. If there was a secret to success I could pass on, it would be to listen to the advice from people who take a genuine and sincere interest in you and your future. They truly have your best interests at heart. Become aware of the signs for opportunity because opportunity is everywhere. Learn from failure. You can always start again tomorrow. And perhaps most of all -- once you've achieved success, be willing to give back as much as you can. If I can give even a fraction of the time and attention those who have impacted my life gave to me, I will feel like I've lived up to Emerson's rule of greatness and done something significant for the world.

Behind the Scenes Takeaway

I interviewed Newy later in the project and was fascinated by how his story honors people from where shaping relationships happen: school, family, work, church and friendship. At a young, influential age, Newy was open-minded about receiving guidance from people who were willing to mentor him with a common theme of believing in himself. These various people, from legends to everyday mentors, encouraged Newy to be the awesome individual he is today. I admire how he has thanked people along the way and gives back so generously through his scholarships.

Key Question for Personal Reflection

As Newy suggested in this story, when was the last time you asked yourself:
why am I doing what I'm doing?

A Pioneer's Legacy

by Lisa Deer

Honoring Dr. Linda Holloway

The goal of parenting is the same, whether your child has a disability or not. It is to raise that child up to be a responsible, healthy, happy person. I believed this when my son Josh was diagnosed with autism in 1997. Because of the incredible work and influence of Dr. Linda Holloway, I believe it even more today.

Linda is the Department Chair for Disability and Rehabilitation at the University of North Texas. She has her Ph.D. in rehabilitation counseling and has been working in this discipline for more than 30 years, a true champion in the field. I first met her in 2008 at a UNT Autism task force I was invited to be part of as a parent representative. We share the same vision and the same ideas about people with disabilities: if you've met one person with autism, you've met one person with autism. Everyone is an individual and deserves to be treated like one.

Linda is a very positive person. I liked her immediately. We both believe all people -- regardless of disability -- should have the chance to be successful in pursuing their dreams and careers, while working and functioning in their communities. Our long-term goal is to reach far back to the transition age which starts in middle school where, if kids can start getting the right kind of help by the time they get to college, a lot of hurdles to their success are already behind them. We'd also like to see a greater number of people without disabilities value the contributions autistic people make to society.

In the time since I've known Linda, we've seen positive gains in this capacity.

But we still have a long way to go.

Autism is a global disorder. It affects people in every race and culture.

There is no one-size-fits-all diagnosis with autism, either, making it particularly overwhelming. What's true for one person with autism may not be true for another. When we received Josh's diagnosis, we were told he would most likely be in a group home for the rest of his life; he couldn't drive; he wouldn't work. I refused to accept that prognosis. Today he drives. He goes to school. He's successful and he works. The journey hasn't been easy, though, and we've relied on a lot of help along the way.

At the time of Josh's diagnosis, the rate of autism was 1 in 10,000 children. Today, it's 1 in 68, with 1 in 42 for boys. In 1997, not much was understood about the condition, and I felt like a pioneer in the wilderness as I searched for answers. With the rate of the incidence of autism growing, I believe a social tsunami is coming. I was looking at the wave saying, "We're not ready. The world's not ready. What's going to happen to them when they grow up?"

Linda saw this wave, too. Of course, I was concerned for my child, but I was thinking about other people's children as well. There will be a whole group of people in the coming years who have existed on the edges of society. Every autistic individual I've met or worked with has been bullied or mistreated, or they've perceived being bullied or mistreated because their own communication skills have been lacking, and it becomes a self-fulfilling prophecy.

This is one of the biggest reasons the work Linda does is so incredibly important. One of her sayings is, "Everyone can work." Work is pivotal to being an adult. Where you work dictates who you spend your day with. Work gives you challenges, and it gives you opportunities to grow and shine at what you're good at. In short, work opens doors for people, both with and without disabilities. But work is especially important to someone with a disability because, otherwise, they end up isolated, sitting at home. Research has shown that 70% of high-functioning adults are at home all day with no work or social activity. This is unacceptable.

The fact is, people with disabilities are talented. They have gifts. They can contribute. If someone recognizes their value and is willing to accommodate the areas that need to be accommodated, magic happens. Companies like SAP, Oracle and Microsoft are recognizing the value of people with autism and what they bring to the table. SAP hires people in work groups, so the people with autism are with their new colleagues from the start. This approach is an asset for everyone. Group leaders learn about each member of the group. They know their quirks and have each other's backs. In short, they *get* them. With this inclusive approach, companies can succeed with employing people with autism and retaining them, while benefiting from the unique talents they bring to the workplace.

This inclusive spirit of seeing each individual's potential and ability to contribute is at the heart of Linda's work. Her passion for finding ways to break down the barriers between people with disabilities and how they are received in society has influenced me to work professionally in this field. She encouraged me to go back to school. She said, "You have so much to offer, Lisa. You could consult, and it would really help to have those credentials behind your name." She made me believe I could do it. Going back to school in my late 40s to pursue a Master's degree was intimidating, despite my love of learning, but I did it. Knowing I have people like Linda supporting me helped, and earning the right training and credentials makes me feel better about the work I do with students.

I am learning even more than I expected.

In fact, the more time I spend with autistic people one-on-one, the more they continue to amaze me. I have students most people would write off. I've worked with students whose families have abused them. Others have been marginalized because they struggle with social skills. The secret is helping them become comfortable enough to be able to shine and bring out their gifts. Everyone can benefit from that. Linda did that for me when she took me under her wing as I was learning the ropes in this field, and I'm thrilled I'm now able to pay it forward.

My ultimate goal is to help autistic people see their own value, their own talents, and how they can contribute, and then to learn how to be other-minded. Autism means "of the self," and it's not that they're selfish -- they often do not recognize the thoughts of others when they're little. Their inability to gain perspective is a huge part of the problem. But when they can work in an intervention program geared toward how they are wired, it's amazing what can happen.

Research shows that engaging in sensory activity increases attention and retention in people with autism. It helps them focus. Autism is generally an impairment in communication skills. We had to artificially teach Josh language. Even though Asperger's isn't technically a term that's used any longer, those of us working in the field will use the term as a descriptor to help pinpoint where someone falls on the spectrum in terms of functioning. People with Asperger's tend not to have the language delay, but they still have difficulty with figurative language. If you say something like, "I have a splitting headache," someone with Asperger's will tell you they envision an axe splitting your head. They are very literal.

The character of Sheldon on the hit TV show *The Big Bang Theory* is a classic poster boy for Asperger's. He is like a lot of my students, although he is more extreme.

One of the men I have worked with is 6'4" and has a deep, gruff voice. The first meeting he came to, he said to me, "May I make a suggestion?"

I said, "Sure, but why don't you tell me your name first? My name is Lisa."

He paused and said, "Oh, my name is Jerry.* I would like to request a diet beverage. I don't see any in the choices available."

I said, "I'm sorry, we don't have any, but I have bottled water and iced tea."

"Well, I don't drink tea and I'm morally opposed to bottled water."

All I could say was, "Well, I'll work on that for next week, but I'm so glad you're here."

It was still the beginning of the meeting; people were still coming in. I needed to go upstairs for something and while I was up there, I discovered a diet soda in the refrigerator.

"Jerry," I said when I came back into the meeting room. "It's your lucky day! Look what I found." I held up the can for him.

He looked at the can, then looked at me. With a deadpan face he said, "Well how desperate are you for approval?"

Most people would be offended by a statement like that. It was all I could do to not burst out laughing. I was thinking to myself, you know, he's kind of right! They call it like they see it.

Autism involves a lot of repetitive behaviors. It often looks like nervous ticks. People with autism have sensory issues. Loud noises bother them. Given this, people with autism usually don't play sports because their gross and fine motor skills can be impaired. Fortunately, that was not the case for Josh. When he was little, he developed a love of sports. He could shoot basket after basket from far away -- 3 pointers. People with autism can have intense focus. When he got into hockey, he would watch Mike Modano of the Dallas Stars, and he would copy his wrist shot.

When he started using his wrist shot in practice, the kids and the coach were blown away. In hockey, there's a shootout at the end of the game if it's tied. The coach would never put Josh in for the shootout because he was afraid if Josh missed, he'd have a meltdown and get embarrassed.

But the other parents and kids said, "Coach, put Josh in!"

So the coach finally did. Josh made the shot. The entire place erupted. Everyone was high fiving on the team, and my husband said, "Did you get that on tape?"

All I was doing was holding my breath and praying, "Don't let him melt down. Don't let him melt down. Don't let him melt down!"

The coach told me later he had to apologize to the other coach because they were celebrating like they'd just won the Stanley Cup.

But this situation showed me, once again, what was possible when given the opportunity.

When Josh was a freshman at UNT, he struggled to make friends. Being a commuter is hard; being a commuter with autism is a lot harder. Programs designed to help adults with autism socialize are few and far between. Funding and support are even scarcer.

During that time, Linda and I discussed the options for starting a program specifically for autistic students on the UNT campus. At that point, we still hadn't been able to make any ground in developing a comprehensive program for people on the Autism Spectrum.

I said, "What can we do with our own resources?"

She said, "How about we start a social group for students with Asperger's and Autism?"

And so, Tuesday Night Flights was born. It was small at first, with only five students. We didn't want to have the word autism in the group's name so as not to stigmatize the members. We called it "Flights" because the mascot for UNT is the eagle, and the goal is for them to fly socially. We would meet for two hours each Tuesday night and it was purely social: to mingle, feel more confident and comfortable, and have friends at school.

Josh loves to eat and he'd become friends with the people who ran the pizza place on the north end of campus. The staff there loved him, so I approached them and asked if they'd consider allowing us to meet there as a group. Not only did they enthusiastically agree, but they even gave me a discount on their pizza! Linda and I personally shared the expenses of buying pizza for the meetings. Most of my students live on a very limited income, and we did not want cost to be a barrier to attendance.

The next semester we moved to a room on campus. Linda was there every step of the way. She saw my talents and I know she truly believed in me. Tuesday Night Flights became the practicum for my master's degree. We maintained five students for the first two semesters, and in the fall of 2014, we grew the group to seven. The following spring semester, we grew it to fifteen people, with an average of 8 attending every week. Each semester we've been able to coach and teach more, but in a subtle and natural way. The students now want to help further the field of autism research and have agreed to be a part of a formal study for their peers.

This semester we are moving to the next level. Tuesday Night Flights is becoming an official student organization. We are now at a place where they are empowered to make decisions about group goals and activities. They are gaining vocational skills in working with others. It's very exciting!

I'm pioneering the research in this area because there's not much like this going on anywhere else. We are out in front of the field, and it arose from a need for my own child, who isn't even at the university anymore. Instead, he is pursuing a degree at a golf school to become an instructor. Last semester he came to the group as a guest and showed the students how he prioritizes and gets organized for his classes. He's become a role model for a lot of students, and it fills my heart to see him succeeding.

Most people attribute Josh's success to my investment in working with him, but there's more to it than just me. Over the years we worked with at least sixty people including behavioral analysts, teachers, therapists and counselors, along with all the other people who have been involved in his life since he was three years old. While all that support was incredible, the common denominator was Josh. He did all the work. He wasn't always happy about it, but he has the heart of a servant leader and he's tenacious. He's also rooted in his faith and he loves people. He wants to please, and he wants to help.

I believe a lot of other "Joshes" are out there who, with the right programs in place, can be as successful and happy as he is.

Today, we collectively know more about autism and how to work with people who have it than at any other time in history. It has certainly improved in the time span since Josh was little. We were told he couldn't do a lot of things, but we didn't let that stop us from setting the bar higher for him and seeing what he truly could do. He surpassed what even we believed was possible, and he continues to go over and above what we had hoped for him. Parents of autistic children do the best they can. Everyone has his or her own individual capacity, opportunity, and resources. I have learned not to judge others as a result of my experiences as a parent of a child with special needs.

Because of Linda, I've made it my life's work to build awareness for people with autism, being a champion for programs designed to advance their lives and help parents. If I were to thank her so she would understand the full extent of how much she has impacted my life, it would be launching the project we've been working on. Seeing our dream come to fruition is the best I can do for her. Certainly she would appreciate receiving a gift, but that's not what she's about. As her career culminates over the next five years, she really wants to see even greater gains in her field. Her research and efforts to advance our understanding of people with disabilities will be part of her enduring legacy, what is truly **a pioneer's legacy**.

Maya Angelou has a quote that I love. She says, "People will forget what you said. They'll forget what you did. But they'll never forget how you made them feel." I will never forget how Dr. Linda Holloway has made me feel, and I aspire to serve others in that way. I'm excited about the work I'm doing and the possibilities people with autism have for making the world a better place. She passed that on to me, and now I'm passing that on to others. I see it working for Josh every day, and as a parent, a professional, a part of the autistic community and society in general, I couldn't be more proud or optimistic about what's in store.

Behind the Scenes Takeaway

When I was interviewing Lisa, I considerably increased my understanding of autism. I never knew, for example, that the word autism means "of the self," which explains why communication can be such a challenge. This made me realize how little the average person might know about the condition. One of the biggest takeaways from her story is the clear need for more opportunities for autistic individuals to work and contribute to society on a larger scale. It was also inspiring to learn that one who believes may not show up when we're young, but instead comes to us later in life the way Dr. Holloway did for Lisa.

Key Question for Personal Reflection

Maya Angelou's quote is very powerful: "People will forget what you said, but they will never forget how you made them feel."
Who in your life comes to mind when you think of this important quote?

A Man of Few Words

by Julia Telligman

Honoring Robert Howery

It was 1992 and I was working at Burlington Northern Railroad at the time. I reported to Robert Howery. He was Senior Vice President of the company and in charge of nine divisions across the United States. He was a gentle giant. When he walked into the room, everyone stopped what they were doing, and he would own the room. In my opinion, he was a powerful and influential businessman, yet he was also soft-spoken. Everything he did and said was intentional.

I've always been a good worker, but some people are just easier to work with than others. There's a connection. Bob was like that. He was a man of few words, but for some reason, I just got him, he got me, and we worked very well together. He liked to tease me that I was always a step ahead of him at work. One of his favorite things to say to me was, "I know you've probably done this, but I have to ask…"

Everything Bob did was impressively purposeful, so when he reached out to me during an especially tough time in my life, I couldn't ignore the wakeup call and opportunity he was giving me for personal growth.

At this time in my life, I was going through a divorce. It was two years in the making as we struggled to get past issues with infidelity and verbal abuse. I could not recover and get my confidence back staying in the marriage. I was beat down by my ex-husband and family to remain married and make it work, but I could not gain the trust and the love I needed to have a happy, healthy life. Bob could not help but see that I was struggling with personal issues as I was walking this path.

One day, Bob handed me a brochure. The brochure was about self-esteem and confidence. Like I said, he was a man of few words, so this was his way of letting me know he cared about me and my situation and could tell I was hurting.

"I think you need to go to this," he said.

Bob was an exceptionally busy person. There was no socializing at all. For him to see my struggle, for him to notice I needed support, let alone reach out to me and offer what he did, was remarkable. He made me realize, "Wow, if he sees this in me, so do a lot of other people." It was a real jolt, one that made me decide I needed to change something in my life.

If the circumstances were different, had even a friend I'd confided in about what was going on in my marriage -- someone who knew me better -- done this for me, I would have dismissed it, brushed it away and said, "Oh, whatever."

But for Bob to do it was something else altogether. He was a giant at work, number three in the company. He had a lot of responsibility in his position. I took the gesture very personally and made the decision to take my life back.

It's been 24 years, so I really don't remember much about the seminar, except it was definitely the wake-up call I needed. I realized I must not have had very high self-confidence because of what I'd been going through, and Bob saw that in me and wanted to help. I walked away from the class armed with some valuable business skills, about being a business woman and having confidence and self-esteem at work.

Right around that same time, I went back to school and finished my degree. I only had about 26 hours left to complete the requirements, and Bob told me about and helped with the tuition assistance program through Burlington Northern. Getting your degree lifts you, as well. It gets you to a point where you say, "I can take care of myself." That was a point I needed to be at, and Bob was instrumental in helping me get there.

I worked for Bob for about two more years. Our relationship stayed on track and professional after I took the class. When I was asked the question, "Who is the one person who believed in you?" My first thoughts went directly to this time in my life, when Bob Howery extended his hand to me and lifted me up. That allowed me to move forward with my life.

I recently reached out to Bob on LinkedIn. It felt great to let him know how much he's meant to me over the years, and as I wrote the words, I felt relief and gratitude rush out of me. It was an amazing feeling! I read what I wrote at least 3-4 times to make sure everything sounded okay before I hit the send button.

"Is this the Robert Howery I worked for at Burlington Northern Railroad?" I wrote.

He responded, "Yes."

I was thrilled and shocked that he replied so fast! When we worked together, technology was challenging for him.

I then wrote him a longer email, asking him how he was doing and about his family. I wrote, "I don't know if you realize it or not, but you made a huge difference in my life." I wanted him to know the important part he played over the years. I don't have issues with confidence or self-esteem anymore. As a result, I was able to create the life I have today. I'm married to a man who really loves me and lifts me up. Had I not addressed my personal issues, I would not have been in the right state of mind and well-being to meet him.

The best part is, Bob wrote back! It meant the world to me to hear from him. He told me he has 13 grandchildren and wrote:

"Great to hear from you and so happy to learn that you found an amazing guy and have a wonderful family. When you worked for me, you did a great job. I knew you were going through difficult times. I am pleased I was able to help when you needed it the most."

To this day, I've carried with me the lessons I learned from that tough time in my life. I am definitely more in tune with people around me and reach out to them with kind words and encouragement. I can think of several people I've met and mentored and helped with their self-esteem and confidence, including my best friend Sherry, whom I met through Tarrant County Junior College. That simple act of reaching out and caring about someone going through a tough time the way Bob reached out and cared about me so many years ago led to us becoming best friends. I lost her to cancer in 2006. We definitely became each other's rock through difficult times in our lives. Over the years, I've stayed in touch with Sherry's daughter, and I've enjoyed keeping the coals of that family connection lit. Somehow, it makes her presence that much stronger in my life.

Thank you, Bob Howery, for being a part of my life, and for demonstrating first-hand the power of a simple act of kindness.

Behind the Scenes Takeaway

When I was interviewing Julia, I noticed how heartfelt she was when she expressed her gratitude for how Robert Howery helped her address a personal issue in a professional manner. During our conversation, she wondered out loud several times if she could actually find him,thank him, and complete the loop. And she did! One of the biggest takeaways from her story is when we are going through difficult times, we are often unaware of our disengagement from regular, everyday life. Staying tuned in and intentional with those around us can ensure open access to tools that can lead them to greater personal growth and fulfillment.

Key Question for Personal Reflection

How can you reach out and help someone get back on track with their life?

The Power of Learning

by John Lee Dumas

Honoring Benjamin Franklin

Multiple people in my life have impacted me in powerful ways. My father. My podcasting mentor. Leaders in the armed forces when I was serving our country on my tour in Iraq and Afghanistan. But if I had to pinpoint the one person who inspires me and is a constant influence in my life, it would be, hands down, Benjamin Franklin.

Obviously, I never knew Benjamin Franklin personally. He was born in 1706 and passed away in 1790. But like so many of this country's great leaders and thinkers, he left his legacy behind in the books he wrote and the things he created. I was eleven years old when I discovered his autobiography, and he came alive for me in those pages. Even though the book is dense and full of big words, it inspired me so much that I decided, from that point on, I would model everything I did after him.

Had it not been for my father reading adult books to me starting when I was four, I probably never would have gravitated toward Ben Franklin the way I did at such a young age. My father has always been a big believer in reading. After graduating from Georgetown with a major in English, his goal was to be a Professor of Literature at an influential university or college. But the Vietnam War was going on and he was presented with three options: be drafted, go to law school, or go to medical school. He decided to go to law school and become a lawyer. He's had his own practice for 35 years, but he never lost his passion for reading and literature even though his career took a different turn. The power and magic of reading was just one of the many things he has passed on to me.

When he read to me, I remember always asking him questions like, "Daddy, what does that mean?" in reference to something I didn't understand.

His reply was consistently the same. He would say, "Hey, that's a good question! If you don't understand something, make sure you ask because there is nothing you are going to get out of not knowing."

This spirit of asking questions and being curious led me to read all kinds of books. Once I found Ben Franklin's autobiography, I tackled that book with Webster's Dictionary by my side. I went through the material slowly because I had to stop and look up words on just about every page. Pacing myself also aided in my digestion and absorption of the content.

One thing I was particularly taken with was the way he described the importance of learning how to adapt to your surroundings. When he traveled to England, for example, he made an effort to adapt himself to the English culture. When he went to France, he adapted to the French culture. I admire this characteristic because I think a lot of people who travel today hold on too strongly to their individual traits and national heritage. Individuality is great, but not at the expense of alienating people around you, especially when visiting another country. I studied for four months in India and that was a huge culture shock for me. I think I would've really struggled had I not been able to say to myself, "Hey, what would Benjamin Franklin do in this situation?" I knew he wouldn't try to impose his American values or culture onto theirs. He would have said instead, "What's special to the people who live here? I'm coming to their country and they're welcoming me and opening their doors to me. What can I do in a really powerful way to become part of this culture, instead of being an antagonist to it?"

Another characteristic I admire in Benjamin Franklin is his courage. As a young man in his late teens, Ben had a falling out with his family. Instead of doing what most people do, which is to eventually crawl back and make amends, he said, "You know what? I'm done with this town." He lived in Boston at the time. He said, "I'm taking off and I'm going to find *my* town. Because no matter what, my family is here, and everything I ever do in Boston is going to echo back to them. I want a completely fresh start."

So he went to Philadelphia, which wasn't at all like going to Philadelphia in 2016 where you can just jump on a 45-minute plane ride. In the early 1700s, going from Boston to Philadelphia was a week-long proposition. He went down there with nothing in his pocket. In fact, when he got off the boat in the new city, all he had was a loaf of bread in his hand. Not even a dollar to his name. But he did have a skill. He knew how to print, and that was critical.

Knowing he had that valuable skill gave him courage. As long as he knew how to print, he believed he would be able to find his way in the world. That was really eye opening for me. Learning at a very early age the importance and value of having a skill, that other people value as well, helped me tremendously as I grew up. I put experiences that came my way through the lens of what Benjamin Franklin might do in whatever situation I happened to be in. Even to this day, I often ask myself, "How can I emulate what he did?" and "How can I gain skills in my life that will make me valuable to other people?"

My podcast, Entrepreneur on Fire, is one great example of how I have applied Benjamin Franklin's principles to my life. When I was looking to launch into the world of entrepreneurship, I thought to myself, "Hey, I really want to be mentored by today's most successful entrepreneurs. What's the best way to do that?" I figured out pretty fast that having conversations with them would be a great route to take. But I also knew that the only way I was going to have conversations with the Seth Godins, Michael Hyatts, and Tim Ferrisses of the world was if I could provide them something of value in exchange for their time and wisdom. After taking the time to explore my options, I discovered the thing I could provide to these great and successful entrepreneurs was a platform where their voice could be heard, not just by me, but by anybody who wanted to listen to the show I was creating.

So I created my podcast, and it has become something of value, not just to me and the entrepreneurs I talk to each day, but to the millions of listeners around the world. Just like Benjamin Franklin knew how to print and run a printing press, I know how to run a microphone, a mixer, and a recording and editing program. I know how to use Skype and call my guests using that free service. I can successfully record, edit and publish our conversations. Through the guided conversations we have, I'm getting the benefit of being mentored by them and they're getting the benefit of having their voice, their product, their service, or community shared with the world. My audience gets the benefit of all of it rolled together.

What's interesting is that podcasting, in some ways, is the 2016 version of the 1740 printing press. Back in 1740, the printing press was the way information was delivered so people could learn, read, and keep up on the news. Today, podcasting is one of the fastest-growing segments of mass communication. Information, news, and the like no longer need to be delivered in a printed, physical form, but can instead be delivered via the airwaves. I think that's an interesting correlation, one that Benjamin Franklin would most likely find interesting, too, if he were alive today.

I've been fortunate to have some of today's most influential entrepreneurs on my podcast. One of the questions I always ask each guest is, "What lessons have you learned from your failures as an entrepreneur to become successful today?" If I could have Benjamin Franklin on the show, I would want to start our conversation with what he considers some of his worst moments growing up. He is a bit flippant in parts of his autobiography about some of the tough times he experienced. I would want to dig in below the surface of what was going on and say, "Listen, I know you struggled. You got off the boat in Philadelphia and all you had was a piece of bread in your hand. You got a job. But I suspect there's more to the story. It would be valuable for listeners to hear how you managed those tough times beyond getting off a boat, walking up to a print shop and getting a job. There is fear and anxiety somewhere in that mix."

Sometimes it's tough to convey those deeper, more vulnerable feelings in the written word. Sometimes you don't want to convey them at all because it is your autobiography and you want to present yourself as tough or having it all together. But I would want to focus tightly on the struggles he had because one of the big inspirations on my show is how every successful entrepreneur has gone through a period of being scared, of thinking they weren't good enough, or doubting they had what it takes to make it. Even after making it, many entrepreneurs continue to struggle with imposter syndrome or feelings of not being worthy of their success. We are human beings, after all. Some pretty serious dips may be just around the corner because this journey of entrepreneurship is a rollercoaster. I imagine Benjamin Franklin experienced his own dips, and I would want to talk through these things with him in more detail on my show.

I'd also want to dive into some of his most well-known phrases and have him elaborate on them. Believe it or not, a lot of people don't know that many of their favorite sayings or quotes can be traced back to Benjamin Franklin. One of my favorites is, "Early to bed, early to rise, makes a man healthy, wealthy and wise." I was reading his book for the third or fourth time when I was just out of college and I remember thinking, "Man, there is obviously something here." I was looking around at my friends who weren't that successful. They were out late at night and waking up late the next morning. Their lives were haphazard, at best. Then I was looking at my friends who were successful and they seemed to have their systems down. They woke up and had a routine. They were getting things done and it was really impressive. That quote caused things to click for me. Yes, it's a simple quote. It rhymes, so a lot of people don't really think about its meaning, but if you dissect it, it's very powerful. I mean, who *doesn't* want to be healthy, wealthy and wise? For me, it was a light bulb moment.

Finally, as we wrapped up our conversation on my podcast, I'd want to say to him, "Listen, Benjamin. You are admired by a lot of people. I know you had a very successful life and you helped form America into what it is today. You invented a lot of useful tools and contributed many insights to our country. But what I really want you to realize is that it's the little things of your life that I studied and really learned a lot from. It wasn't your big inventions like bifocals, the pot belly stove, or the lightning rod that have made a difference to me. Those are all important and you deserve all the recognition you received for them, but it's the small things you've done in life, like keeping up correspondence with people, that I take a keen interest in and believe matter most."

He expresses this idea of keeping things simple in another one of his sayings: "Be humble. Be happy." I love how he equated being happy with being humble. We all want to be happy, so if you want to be happy, be humble. I'm grateful to him for the small insights like this one that add up to be greater insights over time.

Every five years or so, I make a point of re-reading Benjamin Franklin's *Autobiography*. In fact, about a year ago, I actually downloaded the audio book. It was the first time I'd listened to his words. The narrator did a really good job of reading the manuscript. He captured Benjamin Franklin's personality and voice structure as it comes across in his writing. It was a really cool experience, and it gave me a different perspective on the man and his book I've admired for more than twenty years now.

For any number of reasons, some people may not find a role model in their life. This is why it's important for them to know that they always have the power to find their role models in other places -- in books, documentaries, or podcasts, for example. Finding Benjamin Franklin through reading his autobiography definitely changed my life. He helped me understand the value of being a lifelong learner. We may not recognize it right away, but when we don't invest in ourselves, or seek out the wisdom of people who have lived a different kind of life than we have, we lose something precious. Our purpose in life comes from driving toward something bigger than ourselves. That learning, that excitement, that new thing we're going after shapes our lives, giving us meaning. I like to picture that 4 or 5-year-old child whose eyes are full of wonder at every single thing they see. The goal is to never lose that wide-eyed exuberance, to be like a sponge until our very last day.

Benjamin Franklin did that, and lived until the age of 84. He exemplified the power of learning, which is something I strive to incorporate into my life every day. Now that we live in a world of podcasts, audio and Kindle books, not to mention Netflix and Amazon Prime, I believe there are no excuses for not consuming great content every single day. Reading, listening, and watching great stories, lectures, and trainings are all ways we can continue to learn and develop ourselves. If he were alive today, I believe Benjamin Franklin would be thrilled with the advancements in technology and how readily available information is for us to consume and use. He would probably have helped build the Internet.

And he definitely would have a podcast!

Behind the Scenes Takeaway

When I was interviewing John, I was struck by his commitment to life-long learning, curiosity and his passion for Ben Franklin's life. One of the biggest takeaways from his story is that mentors don't necessarily have to be alive. They can come from other sources like books or podcasts where timeless insights are always available for us to apply to our own lives. This opens limitless avenues for people who are searching for guidance and inspiration and may not find it in their immediate circle of influence. I also admire JLD's entrepreneurial spirit to continue being relevant to his audience, Fire Nation.

Key Question for Personal Reflection

What "positive" lessons have you learned from your failures as an entrepreneur (or employee) to become successful today?

The Golden Thesaurus

by Mary Lou Kayser

Honoring Robert "Bob" Feinstein

It was a typical day in late June on Long Island: hazy, hot, and humid. I sat on the front lawn of Northport Junior High School with my ninth grade cohorts, restless and eager to start our much- anticipated, summer vacation. Divots dotted the grass from the clods we picked and threw at each other to make the time go faster. We could all sense how close we were to starting the next chapter of our lives. The only barrier between us and ten weeks of freedom was surviving a mandatory end-of-the-year awards ceremony. As was customary for me at that time in my life, I couldn't have cared less about any of it.

Looking back at that year, I'm not sure I would have made it to the high school had it not been for my English teacher, Robert "Bob" Feinstein.

Bob was a first-year teacher when I showed up in his class. All us kids liked him immediately. He had every characteristic that made a teacher cool in our eyes: a passion for rock n roll music (Bruce Springsteen was one of his favorites); a willingness to take us as we were, even when we were squirrely, foolish, and unfocused; a love and understanding of teenage angst (he was only a few years out of that madness himself); and the patience of a monk when we screwed up. Which we did. Often. Bob approached teaching the prescribed curriculum the way many young teachers do, putting his own spin on getting us through tired classics like Ernest Hemingway's *Old Man and the Sea* and the required grammar lessons designed to prepare us for state tests.

But what Bob did best was give us creative writing assignments. Lots and lots of creative writing assignments, the polar opposite of the boring exposition we'd been forced to write the year before. He gave us fresh, provocative prompts designed to tap into our imaginations and allow us to create without borders. Every now and then, he'd slip into the curriculum a short story or poem he believed was a better example of what we were supposed to learn related to the endless list of district-mandated learning objectives. He was the first teacher who showed us a Beatles song was actually a poem, and that Bob Dylan had insights about humanity that rivaled writers from the literary canon. He encouraged us to experiment with language and see writing from popular culture as a legitimate form of expression.

The timing for me and this kind of classroom could not have been more fortuitous. I now believe the Universe put me in Bob Feinstein's class for one reason and one reason only: to help me find myself again, a self who had been hijacked by peer pressure and hormones and a desperate desire to be loved for who she was, flaws, quirks, extra pounds and all.

You see, 9th grade was the first year since kindergarten when I didn't show up fat on the first day of school. Over the summer between 8th and 9th grades, I'd grown taller and slimmed down considerably, mostly from a combination of walking everywhere, not eating much, and smoking cigarettes. Like many formerly overweight people, however, I still had the mindset of a fat kid, one who'd been teased and bullied for years. So I did the only thing I knew how to do in order to protect this newly formed creature I'd become and was still unfamiliar with: I became best buddies with reckless behavior. Anything that blocked the pain and wonder of my metamorphosis was fair game. Smoking, drinking, cutting class, fooling around with older boys, getting suspended and put in detention for telling the vice principal to f- himself, wearing heavy makeup and long feather earrings that mirrored joint clips you could pick up at the local head shop protected me from a world I believed was mean, cruel, and out to get me. Hostility, aloofness, and sarcasm were my weapons of choice, and I held on to them fiercely.

These things gave me the protection I wanted, but underneath my tough exterior was an exhausted 14-year-old who was tired of carrying their extra weight in her satchel. I longed to ditch them but was too afraid to let them go. Sad, depressed, and scared, I yearned for something to be different so I could just be me. In Mr. Feinstein's class, each new writing assignment gave me the chance to explore my confusion, my secrets, my self-doubts, my dreams. Slowly, carefully, I let my guard down and opened up my world to him on the page. Bob allowed me to be honest, encouraged it even, with his lengthy comments scribbled by hand on each paper I got back, almost always with an A. He was direct with his feedback, guiding my craft with well-constructed observations about where I needed to improve, while pointing out where I had the magic, where my voice really soared. He never once judged, criticized, or shamed me for anything I wrote.

Instead, he rewarded me publicly when he read my writing aloud to the class, always anonymously, of course. It didn't take long for everyone to figure out who the mystery writer was each time he shared a student story. My writing wasn't the only work he shared. Those of us who were consistently featured had distinct styles and voices that modeled what Bob believed was great about our age group -- and great about emerging writers. Heaping gobs of praise on each writer whose pieces he shared didn't divide us; instead, it created a dimension to the community he built inside the classroom that we fiercely guarded and bragged about to friends who didn't have him for their English teacher.

Despite the secret thrill I felt when he read my work to the class, a surge of pride and joy I'd never experienced in school before, my face would turn beet red. I hid my burning cheeks behind my hair, or put my head down on my desk until the performance was over and he was on to the next paper, hoping no one was looking at me and yet secretly wanting everyone to be looking at me and thinking how amazing I was.

In the movie *Billy Elliot*, the scene that gets me every time is when the admissions panelists at the elite dance academy Billy has applied to ask him why he dances. The question comes after Billy has had an altercation in the locker room with another boy, and the committee is wondering if he's fit to be at the school at all.

"Dunno," Billy replies. "I just do. It lights me up inside."

He then gets up and dances the dance of his life, proof before their eyes of his conviction to his art. This performance confirms for them that despite his predisposition towards rage and violence, perhaps he deserves a chance to be at their school after all where skilled professionals can help him channel his misguided energy.

Like Billy, I don't know why I took to writing as passionately as I did my 9th grade year, outside of the perfect storm arising out of my newly minted adolescent body, despair over my mother suddenly working full time outside the home, and having Bob Feinstein as my English teacher. I do know that, like Billy, I needed someone to go to bat for me in my darkest hours when I was smoking and fighting and ditching school to hang out off campus with older kids who didn't have my best interests at heart. Someone who could see beyond the lost teenage girl making really bad decisions and believe in her, regardless of her deeply tainted track record.

So it was, on that last day of 9th grade, as I sat on the lawn in the blistering heat of late spring, more interested in throwing grass clods at boys I liked, that my name was called and the kid next to me was poking me in my ribs saying, "You just won an award!" and looking up at the mock stage, seeing Bob Feinstein standing there with the goofy, lopsided grin I'd seen a million times, beckoning for me to get my butt up there and accept my award. And so it was that I made my way across the patchy lawn, past all my peers, some who liked me despite my worst self, others who couldn't stand me because of my worst self, to receive the award he'd gone to bat for me to win, the writing award for the entire 9th grade class, a new hardcover edition of Roget's Thesaurus with my name engraved in gold letters on the inside faceplate of the book, an award he told me I had earned -- and deserved.

The rest of that day remains fuzzy to me, but I still have and use what I call my **golden thesaurus**. In the years since leaving Bob's class, I've written and self-published several books and authored hundreds of blog posts. I've used writing to gain access to job opportunities, sort through difficult personal challenges, earn money, even fall in love. I've kept a regular journal for more than four decades, and I've passed on my love of language and the power of self-expression to students both young and old in a teaching career I dearly loved.

I made a point to visit Bob every year after leaving home for college 3,000 miles away, even after I got married and became an English teacher myself. He never knew when I might show up, but when I did, he always exclaimed, "Oh my God, I don't believe it! What are you doing here? This is amazing!" and welcomed me unconditionally into whatever he happened to be doing at the time, no questions asked, content to have one of his flock back in the fold to show off, ask questions of, listen to, marvel at.

As time passed and I had a family of my own, our correspondence became more irregular. My visits became further apart. The advent of social media platforms like Facebook and LinkedIn have allowed us to connect virtually, but his open suspicion of and vociferous disdain for habitually posting what he believed amounted to little more than nonsense made it clear we wouldn't be having any meaningful conversations online or swapping funny anecdotes in each other's news feed for friends to like and comment on.

Which is perfectly okay, because I like my memories of Bob just the way they are, from a time before social media, Smartphones and texting took over our lives and stole something precious from the collective human experience. Namely, the chance to form relationships organically, over time, face to face, without being clouded by a gazillion other people who watch and comment on everything we do, or being a swipe of a finger away from never existing at all. Ironically, I learned of Bob's retirement from teaching not that long ago on Facebook where his post -- simply the word "Done" with a photo of a classroom attached -- garnered an outpouring of comments from friends, family and former students far and wide.

Even though I will never be able to show up to his classroom again, I imagine when our paths do cross one day down the road, he will briefly notice my gray hair and lines around my eyes. Then he'll flash me his lopsided grin, remembering as I do that special year in his classroom three decades ago when we were both minting our newest selves and exclaim, "Oh my God. I don't believe it! What are you doing here? This is amazing!"

Behind the Scenes Takeaway

When interviewing Mary Lou, I witnessed first-hand the talent that Mr. Feinstein saw in her, a talent she brought to being co-author of this book. Mary Lou is creative, thorough and clear when she communicates. I saw her eyes light up as she recalled how her teacher influenced her to cultivate her passion for writing. One of my biggest takeaways from her story is that high potential talent may not always show up looking the way we might expect it to. Seeing beyond the rough exterior to the vein of gold hidden below the surface without shame or judgment is a responsibility for leaders across industries, not just in education.

Key Question for Personal Reflection

Take a moment and think about someone who may have gone to bat for you.
When have you done that for someone?

A Different Path to Success

by Bibop Gresta

Honoring Mentors of Innovative and Disruptive Thinking

I love disruption and I've always chosen to be strange. Growing up in Italy, I was exposed to traditional ways of thinking and doing things. I've worked hard since leaving home to create a blue ocean in a place where there were only red oceans. A red ocean is where all the sharks swim and there's a lot of competition. A blue ocean is where you can swim without competition. That's why I say, be strange! When you're out of the ordinary and doing the opposite of what people expect, you're always creating something new.

My predisposition for innovative thinking is what led me to become the Chairman and COO of Hyperloop Transportation Technologies, a hi-tech company dedicated to doing things differently. At our core, Hyperloop is about developing transportation options between major cities at lightning speed. It's based on technology that's been around since the 1870s but never got off the ground for a number of reasons. Our solutions propose to solve one of the greatest challenges of our time: moving massive numbers of people quickly and efficiently so cities aren't congested and cars aren't continuing to pollute our environment. The Hyperloop is not only about achieving speeds up to 760 mph with the capsule, it's also about creating a transportation system that uses renewable energy, producing more electricity than it consumes. The amazing fact about the Hyperloop is not only that it is financially efficient, it's efficient in how it works, too. I work with 520 scientists from 42 countries. These facts make the Hyperloop one of the most disruptive ideas of our time.

Looking back on my life, I can see how each of my experiences leading up to running Hyperloop was like being in a gym where I was preparing for what this project demands of me daily. Having the right mentors along the way as I trained and practiced was a critical part of my growth and development. Everything I do today with Hyperloop Technologies draws on their collective influence, along with past work I've done in engineering, company organization, finance and art. It's rewarding to combine all the things I'm passionate about into one project.

Over the years, I selected my mentors based on the kind of situation I was in or the specific problem I needed help solving. I looked for people who were successful in their field, and each one made a difference. I wouldn't say I was lucky because I don't believe in luck. I would say I was able to choose the right path at the right time through a combination of my own innate curiosity about the world and exposure to exceptional mentorship. I believe life is made up of different phases, and we need to have a mentor for each one.

I was 28 years old when I sold my first company, writing a page in the history books of Italy's new economy. In the mid-1990s, I hosted programs on MTV and produced 21 records and six number-one hits on the Italian dance chart. After that, I founded my incubator Digital Magics with my friend Enrico Gasperini and began investing in startups. Overall, I invested in 70 companies. During those early years of my professional life, I did three IPOs in Italy, Germany, and the U.K. My investments ranged from amusement parks to hotels to media companies. Life was good, and I enjoyed the rewards of my hard work.

But like all entrepreneurs, I've known my share of failures and challenges along with the big wins. Some of my ventures were wildly successful, while others didn't work out well. In 2012, I was no longer living the rock star life of a successful businessman who sold companies and made records. I wasn't living in my dream home with every amenity at my fingertips. No, in 2012, I was sleeping in my car as I clung to what was left of my dreams. At that time, I had a million dollars in stocks, but I couldn't sell them because I was having trouble with my business partner and was locked out of my assets. Technically, I was broke.

I was 41 years old.

During that difficult time, I could have renounced my dreams and chosen to go back to Italy. It would have been easy to give up and move on. But when you're sleeping in your car, you have a lot of time to reflect on every decision you've ever made, both good and bad. I realized that my situation was temporary, and I had the power to choose what I wanted to do next. I drew strength to keep going from the memories of my mentors and past successes. I played the movies of those memories and what they'd taught me a thousand times in my head. Doing that kept my hopes up and my dreams alive. I was determined to succeed again, no matter what, believing deep down that my next success was just around the corner, and I could get back on my feet.

I have my father Rino Gresta to thank for starting me down the path of disruption and innovation I've been on my entire life. He was an early influence as I was growing up in Italy, and I admired his capacity to become the leader of every situation he was in. It was incredible to see that happen. As a boy, I looked up to him for guidance and wisdom.

He was strict about his things, though, and said, "Never touch my keyboard and never touch my computer." Strangely enough, telling me *not* to touch his things fueled my curiosity for them, igniting the first sparks of my passion for doing the opposite of what everyone else was doing. Not only did I touch his computer and keyboard, but I became a programmer and a musician. I believe we can learn from doing the opposite of what we're told as much as we can learn from following directions. Our mentors can play a significant role in that process of discovery, leading us to great success.

I was twenty years old and attending university when I got my first taste of educational mentorship from my professor, Antonio Meneghetti. Dr. Meneghetti was a psychologist, and he was very smart. He told me one day, "Don't focus, Bibop."

I was initially shocked and confused about this advice. Everyone else was telling me to focus. Wasn't narrowing down my area of interest the surest way to becoming successful?

"You're too young to focus," he said. "Try new things. Experiment. Fail. Be curious about what you're going to do. You can't possibly decide what that is right now. If you *do* decide on something, you're probably being pushed by someone else. Your father. Your family. Your teachers. Your social environment. Your priest. But not yourself. You will be something when you decide you've seen enough, tried enough, wronged enough, and failed enough. So, don't focus right now."

That's about the wisest advice anyone could give to a twenty-year-old, and I took it to heart. It's exactly the opposite of what society is telling young people today. These days, young people are being told to focus. I believe this is a mistake. Not focusing on one thing allowed me to have a variety of experiences, which in turn formed the bedrock of every decision

I made, including founding my own company, which would make me rich before I turned 30.

I owe that early financial success to Professor Meneghetti as well because he taught me the logic of money.

"If you understand the logic of money," he said, "you can actually control it and make it work for you. If you don't understand it, you have to work for it and it will control you."

Dr. Meneghetti also taught me how human beings think, especially how memes and memetics work to shape the way we see the world. A meme comes from the social learning theory that suggests humans learn best through imitation. The word meme translates from the Greek and means "imitation." A meme is basically information copied from one person to another through things like habits, skills, songs, and stories. Understanding human thought and behavior through the lens of memetics has been extremely useful for my career as a creator and innovator. I've been able to steer clear of trends and buzzwords that don't serve my vision for a better world, and form alliances with people who share my disruptive view of what the world can be like.

Another mentor at the beginning of my career was a man named Dr. Robert Procter. Dr. Procter was a scientist at the University of Canada. I was a young kid on his team developing software for his multi-national company and was eager to learn everything I could. The amazing thing about this man is he had experienced a major failure, yet he didn't allow it to stop him from achieving his goals.

His passion was flying planes, and he had been a pilot. Because of a flying accident in Italy, however, he lost his ability to fly. This turn of events didn't stop him from living his life. Even though he could no longer follow his passion, the important lesson I learned from his story is you have to pursue your dream even if something stops you temporarily. He showed me it's still possible to work toward new goals and achieve success, no matter what obstacles might stand in your way, when you believe in them strongly enough.

Dr. Procter's mentorship helped me when I was building and selling companies. It also helped me when I was faced with the unfortunate situation of firing 200 people, half of whom were my friends. That was really hard, but the experience taught me the value of people and why investing in them makes good business sense. I'm proud that through my companies and projects over the years, I've created jobs for more than

1000 people and given them a chance to succeed. We've struggled through the tough times and come out the other side stronger and more resilient.

A third influence in my entrepreneurial career is my friend Dickie Cessna. Dickie was 17 years old and living on a farm in an isolated area of Australia when he made his discovery. He wanted to create a business, but for the longest time, he was stumped about what kind of business he could form given his seemingly limited circumstances. Every day he'd look out his window and see nothing but cows and, for lack of a better word, their shit.

One day, Dickie came up with the brilliant idea to start selling cow shit, or as Americans call it, manure. He eventually became a billionaire. Today he sells helicopters, but that's how he got his start -- in cow shit. His story taught me the power of perseverance along with the notion that solutions to our most pressing problems are often right in front of us if we simply take the time to look around. They may not look like what we originally imagined, but success is often grounded in how we look at things. When we investigate what's in our immediate environment, and if we can imagine the step-by-step process we need to take to get there, success is a real possibility.

But steps can't be skipped. That's the secret. No fast forwarding to success. Sometimes part of the process is unpleasant, like staring at cow manure all day, firing friends, or sleeping in your car temporarily as you try to figure out how to get back in the game. Each of my mentors taught me this lesson in their own way, and I'm a better man for it.

Turns out, sleeping in my car instead of returning to Italy was a good decision. Most people would have given up and gone home. I decided to do what I've always done and fight for my dreams. Since I can remember, I've gone against the grain. My path looks more like a zigzag than a straight line. I've been successful because I've followed my passion, not someone else's idea of what success means, which is a reflection of the mentors I've had in education, business, family and friendship. That path was certainly different from the majority, but it led me to many achievements.

I haven't had the chance to thank any of my mentors in person. I know I would first embrace them. I'm a physical person and I like people. I would then share with them the practical results their mentorship has allowed me to experience. I think hearing how what they taught me has shaped my life would be the biggest success for them. I imagine they would be proud. They inspired me to learn, grow, fail, and succeed.

Because of my mentors, I continue to give back and pass on my unique perspective on disruption. I'm involved with the JumpstartFund, an organization dedicated to allowing anyone to put the best minds together to solve problems. We use a crowdsourcing approach that may or may not include money to achieve goals. When you want to solve a problem, what you need is people. I've been involved for two years. My favorite part of this project is changing lives and creating a better future for our children. It's a platform that has the potential to solve big problems.

Moving forward, we need to think differently. The new generation is better at this than we are because they care deeply and see a bright future. Through my work and dedication to disruption, I hope I can be a mentor to this next generation, making a difference and shaping the way the world works for many centuries to come. If everyone does his part, this world *can* be better. I'm excited to be a part of that future and plan to contribute for as long as I can to improving the human condition through innovation and a different way of thinking about what's possible.

Behind the Scenes Takeaway

Normally when I use Skype for interviewing, I close my eyes and turn the camera function off because it helps me focus on what my interviewee is saying. What made my interview with Bibop unique was he had the camera function on, and I could see him during our interview. Seeing Bibop as he answered my questions added a new layer to the experience. The irony of this is, it disrupted my thinking and I had to adapt! His willingness to pursue ideas that seem impossible to the rest of us is inspiring. I also admire how he is using today's technology as a way to bring great minds together to solve problems. He has embraced a new way of doing things which will benefit generations to come.

Key Question for Personal Reflection

What path have you taken that was different from what was expected? How did it work out for you?

One Hot Night

by Eddie Gossage

Honoring Howell Lee "HL" Gossage and Bruton Smith

One day, I was walking through the stands at the Texas Motor Speedway with my childhood friend Gary. We grew up together in Nashville, Tennessee, and both come from humble beginnings. Gary is a lawyer today, and I'm the President of TMS in Fort Worth. People in the crowd were hollering, "Hey Eddie!" as we walked along. I was smiling and posing for pictures.

Gary nudged me and said, "2713 Noonan."

Mentioning the address of the home where I grew up is his code for saying, *Man, look how far you've come!*

"Seriously, they give you the keys to this place or something?" he continued.

I waved to the crowd and without missing a beat, I said, "Let me just tell you something. *Somebody* has to be in charge of this place. Why not us?"

He laughed and shook his head. "Why not us?"

I believe everyone should have that attitude. Why shouldn't you be the one who gets to be in charge? Or take the trip? Or go for the dream? If you put in the hard work, you should be rewarded. And let me tell you, I've worked my tail off to get what I have.

I forged the iron of my work ethic in the fires of the example set by two particular men: my dad, Howell Lee "HL" Gossage, and my mentor, Bruton Smith, the founder of Speedway Motorsports, Inc., a company which owns eight NASCAR tracks that host twelve NASCAR Sprint Cup events each year. Each had a hand in making me the person I am. Each gave me opportunity, encouraged me, and corrected me as I made my way in the world. I owe the amazing life I have to both men, and I am honored to have the chance to honor them in this story.

My dad and Bruton were alike in some ways and very different in others. The biggest similarity they share shows up in my desire to never disappoint them. I've been motivated since I can remember to do the right thing, first by my dad and then by Bruton. I never wanted to do anything that would let my dad down. Whether it was playing sports or my performance in school, I wanted my dad to be proud of me. My dad had the unspoken ability to make it clear a person wasn't being respectful if he smoked or drank or lied. Bruton created that same unspoken expectation for me to show up every day and do my best during the nearly thirty years we have worked together. My biggest fear for as long as I can remember is letting either man down. I work very hard to make sure that doesn't happen.

One of the biggest differences between my dad and Bruton is in their professional lives. Put simply, Bruton became a self-made billionaire and my dad worked hard labor his whole career. There are certain people in life who have that Midas touch. Whatever they touch turns to gold. Bruton had that touch, and it was amazing to watch. My dad was one of the hardest working men I've ever known. It was amazing to watch him, too.

I met Bruton Smith in 1989 when I went to work for him in Public Relations at the Charlotte Motor Speedway. Not only has he seen me in my professional prime, but he has been a central figure in shaping what has been a rewarding and successful career for me. In the beginning of my PR career, he was merely an acquaintance. That all changed in 1992 when I accidentally lit him on fire.

To expand racing opportunities at CMS, we decided to put lights in at the track. That may sound like a simple task, but it had never been done at a superspeedway. It was a huge project, and it required several considerations, including how all that light would affect the drivers and how television cameras could get great lighting around the racetrack so fans at home would have a terrific viewing experience.

Before its official launch, we ran some tests with the new light system. The public had been following the project's progress and was chomping at the bit to see it in action. We decided, why not let people come out and see the test run? We didn't think it would be a big deal. Imagine our surprise when close to 65,000 people showed up -- on a weeknight! With that kind of turnout, we knew we had a hold of lightning in a bottle with the fans.

I knew the media would be there because of the hype around the new lights, so I had the guys in the shop build a big box with switches and big thick cables for a publicity stunt. When dusk came, Bruton walked up to the box while the crowd counted down, 3-2-1. On zero, he threw the switch to turn the lights on and pyro shot out from the top of the box. I was standing about six feet from him. TV cameras were closer to him than I was.

The pyro went up and up, and then it started to drop. The next thing I knew, Bruton was on fire. Bruton has white hair, and the top of his head was black. The beautiful sports coat he wore was singed and burned. I couldn't stop thinking, *Oh my God. I've just set the billionaire owner on fire and embarrassed him in front of 65,000 people and worse -- all those TV cameras and photographers!* What was even worse than that, he knew I was the guy responsible for this stunt.

Thankfully, he weathered through it. When it was over, I put my arm around him and said, "Mr. Smith, we tried this earlier today and it worked just fine. I'm sorry we embarrassed and hurt you."

The theme for the race that evening was "One Hot Night." He looked at me and said, "You're taking that one hot night theme a little too far, aren't you?" Then he laughed and stepped through the fence, got in his car, and drove himself to the hospital to have the burns on the top of his head checked out and treated.

The next morning, the Charlotte Observer published a big photograph on the front page. It was a shot taken from behind us, and I've got my arm around Bruton. We're looking at each other and smoke is coming off his head. My first thought was, *I would fire me for this.* I went into work that day prepared for the worst. When I saw the guy who runs the speedway, I asked him what he thought I should do?

He said, "Make a joke about it. He's got a great sense of humor."

So I sent Bruton a little, kitchen fire extinguisher and wrote a note about how much I enjoyed one hot night with him. A little while later my phone rang, and my secretary told me Bruton wanted to talk to me. He'd never called me before.

Here it is, I thought. *The axe is about to fall. Better get a box and start packing up my stuff.*

"May I ask you a question?" he said.

"Sure," I said, bracing myself for the bad news.

"I have friend in Hawaii who saw the show last night. How do you think he saw it?"

I inhaled deeply. "Well, I hired a television crew that shot the highlights from last night. They edited them down and sent them up via satellite from our infield to every TV station in the country."

He said, "How many TV stations are we talking about?"

"Every last television station in the country."

He said, "You're promoting races with satellites. How much did that cost?"

I'm thinking he's thinking, *You used my money to embarrass me.*

"Six hundred dollars," I finally said.

"Six hundred dollars?" he said, disbelief oozing from his voice.

"Yes, sir."

Without hesitating, he exclaimed, "You may be a genius! That is amazing!"

I was dumbstruck. Bruton Smith wasn't going to fire me! In his eyes, I was using space age technology to promote his business to the entire country. His method of promotion involved walking around the local town tacking posters on telephone poles.

I've been his guy ever since.

For close to thirty years, we've had a great run together. Bruton was my boss all that time, but he's also been my friend, my counselor, my MBA professor, my advisor, a comedian and everything else you could think of. There are no boundaries to what we can talk about. We probably talk more about personal things than we talk about professional things.

The public perception of Bruton is a tough, gruff businessman, but privately, he is sweet, funny and brutally honest. He wants what he thinks is fair. In fact, he stopped me from going through with a couple of lawsuits that would have brought the company a lot of money. He said, "You're a good guy, Eddie. If you go through with this, you will put them out of business. Do they really deserve that?"

Here's the odd thing: in all the years I've worked for him, he's never specifically told me to do anything. He takes an indirect approach to giving me direction, calling me and saying things like, "Hey kid. If I was running that big old speedway down there in Texas, I might look into such and such. I might do so and so."

That's his way of telling me he'd like me to do whatever it was he suggested -- without actually telling me. The great thing about this approach is he leaves me with my dignity and isn't ordering me around. I once said, "I work for you," and he quickly corrected me and said, "No, we work *together*."

I've delivered some awful news to Bruton over the last 25 years; I've also delivered some great news to him. But I've always told him the truth, and he's never been mad at me for delivering bad news. No matter what, we always talked about what we were going to do next. We figured things out between us.

I heard Bruton tell my son one time, "Your dad is the most honest guy I've ever met." I was very proud of that because I wanted that to rub off on him.

I could not have asked for a better boss.

I owe my experiences with Bruton to my dad and his influence on me growing up. Even though we were very different, and didn't see eye to eye on a lot of things, I learned several valuable lessons from him over the years and respected him as my father.

My dad was born in 1927. He dropped out of school in 9th grade to join the Navy and fight in World War II. Like so many from the greatest generation, he never told us anything about his experiences in the service. I remember as a little kid seeing his Navy whites and sailor's hat hanging in a closet. They symbolized for me his commitment to servant leadership and doing the right thing.

When he came back from the war, he didn't finish school and was one of those veterans looking for a job, trying to return to a normal life. He eventually found a job working for a packing house in Nashville. He married my mom, whose name was Lucille, and they settled into post-war, blue collar suburban life and had three sons. I'm the middle of three brothers.

Dad worked hard labor for more than 25 years. Along the way he joined and eventually became the President of the Labor Union Local in Nashville. That covered middle Tennessee and southern Kentucky. Eventually, he went to work full time as a business manager for the union until he retired. So after decades of busting his tail as a blue-collar laborer, he climbed the ladder and became a white-collar leader.

Dad didn't make a lot of money, but we had a house and enjoyed family vacations. He bought a used boat and a used camper, and we would go to the lake and camp on weekends. Sometimes we'd get an entire week in the summer. We fished and skied and explored the outdoors. We did without a lot of things, but it didn't matter. When I went off to college, I didn't have a car. I imagine it broke my folks' hearts that they couldn't provide some of the finer things they wanted to give to me and my brothers, but life was good and I've got no complaints. For me, my childhood was perfect.

I had to pay my way through college, and in the summer I worked either construction or in the packing house to earn money. This is when it became clear to me I was not cut out for the same life my dad had lived. Working in a packing house, you're inside and you don't know if it's day or night. I remember thinking, *Good Lord, Dad did this for 25 years.*

Construction wasn't much better. One day, I was five stories up on a scaffold. It was one plank wide, and I was rolling a wheelbarrow full of mortar. *This isn't me*, I thought. *I can't do this! God bless those who can, but I have zero skills with a hammer or a screwdriver.*

I wasn't looking down my nose at the work; I just knew I wasn't cut out for hard labor. A couple of summers in the packing house and then another couple of summers doing construction when it felt like it was 2000 degrees outside was enough for me. Those were great motivators to do something else. My whole goal at college became to not do physical labor. I didn't have any specific profession in mind, but I knew I was designed to do something with my mind more than with my hands. In hindsight, I can see how these experiences were the perfect catalyst for preparing me to work with Bruton.

My dad had a hard time understanding my work in public relations. In the early part of my career, I was running what is now called Bristol Motor Speedway. One time, my dad came to a race and was watching me work. He got to talking to a guy named Ed Clarke, the President of Atlanta Motor Speedway.

My dad said, "Ed, you know I don't see him working. What's he doing?"

Ed said, "What do you mean?"

Dad said, "He's just walking around, talking to people and shaking hands."

Ed said, "Well, Mr. Gossage, is the traffic off the road outside?"

"Yes."

"Are people in their seats?"

"Yeah."

"The concession stands -- they got long lines at them?"

"No, they're just normal."

"And the rest rooms? They got long lines?"

"No."

"Are they clean?"

"Yeah."

Ed said, "Well, that's what he does."

Despite Ed's thorough explanation of my job, my dad still struggled with my choice of profession. To him, if you didn't have sweat running off your nose, you weren't working. I'm not sure he ever fully understood how what I do to make a living is as honorable as what he did. He died before we got Texas Motor Speedway running successfully. Unlike Bruton, my dad never saw me in my prime.

My dad and I became closer the older I got, and also when I got divorced. Things changed between us after that. Dad and I had longer, deeper talks about life. He became more encouraging about my personal and professional life than he had ever been. My only regret is Dad and I had only 14 short months between my divorce in November 1997 and his death at the end of December 1998.

Not long after he passed, I started hearing his voice in my head every single day. I don't know if guilty is the word, but I sure felt badly about not letting him know how important he was to me. He was so much more important than I ever acknowledged to myself. Perhaps that's one of the reasons why Bruton became a fatherly force in my life. With Bruton, I was able to make up for the lost opportunities I could have had with my dad.

Like everyone's life, I've had my share of problems. My marriage ended after twenty years. I had cancer. I lost my mom and then my dad too soon. But I also realized some time ago that my life is better than I ever dreamed it could be. I've done more than I ever hoped I could. I've met presidents and I've flown the Goodyear Blimp and I've gone bobsledding. I grew up admiring Richard Petty and became best friends with his son Kyle. Turns out, Richard is no different than any other dad of any of my other friends -- except for the 200 wins thing.

What made Bruton turn over our company's biggest project to build a speedway with very little direction to a 34-year-old greenhorn? I have no idea, but thank God he did! I suppose the stars aligned perfectly that day because we have had unparalleled success with the speedway since then. No one had opened a speedway that big. Nobody had sold as many tickets or had as big a sponsorship as we did. We set the standard for everything.

When we opened, we were bigger than Daytona was when they opened. We were bigger than Indy when they opened. We were bigger than Charlotte when they opened. To this day, we sometimes draw a crowd bigger than NASCAR in some seasons.

I'm fortunate that I get to do something fun every day and get paid well for it. My friendship with Bruton means the world to me. I've told him how much I appreciate him. I love him with respect, admiration and care. He's told me he loves me, too. He's been sick with cancer and that's been really tough on me. Bruton is 89 now. I've had the chance to thank him in ways I wasn't able to thank my dad when he was still alive. For that, I'm grateful.

When I look back on it all, I realize the luckiest thing I ever did in my life was set Bruton Smith on fire.

Behind the Scenes Takeaway

When I first sat down with Eddie, he was so intrigued with the concept of this project, he began the interview by asking *me* questions! At one point during our conversation, he said he wished we had more time because in our busy lives, how often do we take the time to sit down and talk about the people who have shaped and influenced us? His story also shows how even mishaps don't have to mean the end of the road for us. There's always a way to move past what goes wrong with hard work, passion, and grace.

Key Question for Personal Reflection

Describe a time when you used hard work,
passion and grace to move past
something that went wrong.
How did this experience impact you?

Bronko, a Symbol of Love

by Karen Lopez McWilliams

A Daughter's Story Dedicated to Her Parents

Nicknames are big in my family. We were all assigned our own, special name. My older sister Kathy's nickname was Bouncy because she had a cute, nervous knee twitch. My other sister Kristy was Drifty because she accidentally scored a basket for the opposing team. My younger brothers, John Patrick and David, were called J.P. and Porky, respectively. J.P. came about by combining our parents' first name initials. Porky was chosen because Dave looked like the little boy from the TV show "The Little Rascals." I was nicknamed Bronko, and for the longest time, I didn't understand why.

The name comes from a gentleman named Bronko Nagurski, who was a professional football player for the Chicago Bears from 1930 – 1937. Bronko Nagurski was known as a really tough player when the national football league was being developed. He was tenacious and is considered a legend. The Football Writers Association of America honored him, and a movie called *Hearts in Atlantis* portrays a dramatic monologue of a fictionalized eyewitness account of his 1943 comeback. He worked hard, he had a solid reputation, and he did really well as a player. His legacy was solidified when he was inducted into the pro football Hall of Fame.

Turns out, my dad couldn't have picked a better nickname for me, given the circumstances of my childhood. I was born with a serious eye condition called strabismus, a vision disorder in which a person cannot align both eyes simultaneously under normal conditions. One or both of the eyes may turn in, out, up or down. In 1964, finding a doctor who specialized in correcting strabismus was very difficult. I needed three surgeries at a very young age, and my parents had to look far and wide to find a qualified physician to conduct the procedures. I was less than one when I had my first surgery; I was two when I had my second surgery, and I was a young teenager when I had my third.

Because of depth perception issues, I fell down a lot and was very clumsy when I was a young girl. Despite my awkwardness, I always got back up again and was a very happy, carefree child. Witnessing my tenacious spirit in the face of constant adversity, Dad decided Bronko was a good nickname for me. He would say, "Bronko, hey Bronko!" with such love and positive energy that no matter what my adversities were, no matter what my challenges or handicaps were, I felt special. The name Bronko itself meant I was special. Whenever I heard him call me Bronko, I would jump to it as if reporting for duty. During first and second grade, I didn't want to be called Karen anymore. When my mom or dad called me Karen, I would say, "No, my name is not Karen. My name is Bronko."

Things changed when I became a teenager. The name wasn't a big deal when I was a little girl, but as a teenager, the name bothered me. As I got older, I didn't want to be called Bronko anymore because I felt insulted. I remember thinking sarcastically (as only a teenager can), "Oh wow, that is flattering. My dad has nicknamed his daughter after a football player. I must be fat. Whatever." Dismissing it was easier than trying to understand its meaning. Nevermind asking my dad why he chose to nickname one of his girls after an old football player! The day I finally made the time to ask him about this wouldn't arrive for several decades. For years leading up to that day, I didn't appreciate or respect my nickname the way I do now.

With time comes wisdom, though, and I am certainly no exception to this universal truth. Turns out, calling me Bronko was not just a term of endearment from my dad, but also a deep and profound **symbol of the love** he had for me as a girl who faced more than her fair share of challenges. I didn't like to look people in the eye because of the thick glasses I had to wear and the way my eyes moved while they were getting corrected. I was terribly self-conscious about all of it. When I went in for checkups and exams, I remember feeling intimidated in the doctor's office by the big machines. I distinctly remember not wanting anyone to pay attention to me. I hated that I needed attention from the doctor.

Pre and post-surgery, I had to wear patches on my eyes and glasses that either fell off my face or were lopsided. I felt picked on about how I looked, and despite my parents telling me I was the happiest kid you would ever know, the teasing affected my developing and fragile self-esteem.

Thankfully, my parents were both influential in helping me through this particularly challenging time. They both loved me unconditionally and have been there for me through thick and thin, even to this day. As a girl, I was attached to my mom's hip and didn't want to be away from her side. I remember one day when I was in kindergarten, she had to report for jury duty. You would have thought my world had come to an end! Oh the tears! My dad traveled a lot for business, so he wasn't around as much as my mom; perhaps that's why, as a young person, I never realized how much he cherished me.

Dad worked three jobs in order to pay for my eye surgeries, my very thick prescription glasses, and my doctor appointments. This was one of the driving reasons behind why he was gone as much as he was, and why I didn't see him a lot when I was a young girl. I didn't realize until later in life that working as much as he did was for me and to help pay to correct my condition.

During a family trip to New York in 2014, I had an enlightening conversation with my dad that would change my perception forever. At one point while we were talking, he let out a deep sigh followed by a heavy breath and said, "Karen, I worked so hard when you were a baby." I remember my eyes tearing up, thinking, *Oh my God. Now I understand why my dad had to have three jobs. He did that for me.*

It just never hit me until that moment.

When I returned home, I searched online for information about Bronko Nagurski. Words like "tenacious," "tough," and "a fighter" popped off the page. From that point on, I began to comprehend the true nature of my nickname, that it means far more than a simple reference to an old football player. Dad chose the name Bronko for me because I've been a fighter, I've been tough, and I've gotten through a lot of challenges in my life. I now recognize that I got through those challenges successfully because, deep down, I was aware my dad believed in me.

Not long after that, I called him and finally asked the question:

Why did you give me the nickname Bronko?

His voice became excited and almost childlike. He said, "Karen, when you were born, I wanted a boy so much. I loved football. I would watch you play, and I would watch you run, and you reminded me of a legendary football player named Bronko Nagurski. You would fall and you would get right back up again. It was so cute. What started as a funny nickname turned out to be so much more meaningful as you grew up and faced the challenges with your eyes and your surgeries.

"Now you are an adult and your nickname is so perfect because you've tackled many challenges and struggles – not only personally, but also as an entrepreneur. You've always been a winner, and I am really proud of you."

My heart was beating fast as tears of joy filled my eyes. *My dad just told me he is proud of me!* I thought. Those words struck a deep chord within me.

He told me that as time passed, the name became even more important to him because he worked hard and got right back up, too, when things got tough, just like I did. I was an inspiration to *him*. Hearing him tell me these things was a gift from God, one I will keep for the rest of my life. I'm so glad I asked the question because I never knew! Now, more than ever, I realize my parents have always been proud of me, and it's great knowing I've not just lived up to their expectations, but I hope I have exceeded them.

I'm glad I finally asked my dad about my nickname. His answer became the missing puzzle piece that helped me feel closer to my parents, especially my dad. My parents did a great job because I'm doing well. If it hadn't been for my nickname, along with their love and encouragement, I'm not sure I would have the inner strength I have to overcome today's challenges. The biggest takeaway for me is my parents believed in me throughout my life. As children, we don't necessarily know if we measure up to their hopes. I learned through that phone call that my dad has always loved and believed in me. He saw the neat things I did.

Now, whenever I hear my dad say, "Hey Bronko! How are you?" I smile because I understand the significance of this name to me and my dad. I've started signing my letters to him "Bronko." I've come to love and appreciate the meaning. I don't think I've thanked him for always believing in me. I've not told him directly how special it is he nicknamed me Bronko, especially during those formative years when I needed that energy and excitement to keep me moving forward. I hope this story will show him how much his belief in me means.

Not too long ago, I was visiting with my mom, and she was going through her hope chest. We found several pairs of the cat eye glasses I had to wear when I was two and three years old. She had carefully wrapped my 50-year old glasses in tissue paper. It meant so much to me that she would keep them all these years. Now that I understand the whole story better, they mean that much more to me. I now have them on display in my curio cabinet.

I'm grateful to be named after Bronko Nagurski and hope I can inspire others to be a fighter and never give up. If there's anything I would perpetuate from this experience, it would be how I think about challenging times. When life gets tough, I find myself thinking, *Bronko will win. I will get through this. That fighter in me is going to succeed, no matter what. I'm going to make it.* I think of my dad's voice, and I know everything is going to be fine.

Behind the Scenes Takeaway

After the phone call with my dad, I realized the parent-child relationship evolves as we get older and how important it is to talk about, reflect upon and remember the past. I believe with mutual appreciation, respect, and honesty, the relationship with our parents will become even more meaningful over time. With the demands of today's world, it's too easy to get distracted and, thus, forget to do the little things that matter in the long run that strengthen and build these very important family relationships. Little things can mean a lot. I want to encourage other parents to imagine what their children are thinking or going through and to always make sure you tell them along the way -- no matter how old they get -- how proud of them you are. Let them know so there's never a doubt.

Key Question for Personal Reflection

How have your perceptions of a person of influence in your life changed over the years?

My Final Thoughts and A Call to Action

I hope this book has made you stop, think, and remember the one(s) who really made a difference in your life. I imagine these reflective stories will stir, rekindle, and bring to mind those who have helped you become who you are today.

Take a moment to reflect on your life and ask yourself these questions:

Is there someone in your life who has positively impacted and influenced you? If so, who would it be and why?

One main person may come to mind, or many people. Was it a teacher or counselor? Someone from your family or church? A business colleague or mentor? A neighbor or a friend? Was it a historical figure?

Perhaps you were down on your luck, unsure of life's course and you needed a ray of hope. Or maybe you were full of life and energy, involved in a project where your passion showcased your talents and unleashed your potential.

Perhaps the stars aligned at a critical time and you met a person that positively influenced you to be who you are today! They probably recognized your skills, talents and natural gifts before you even knew you had them. This is why "The Ones Who Believed" is a simple yet powerful consideration for us all!

Upon reflection, some people know exactly who "their one" is right away, while others take more time to pinpoint that special force. Often people identified many individuals from different stages in their life. As the author, I witnessed each story unfold with careful thought, raw feelings and a noticeable, distant reflection of a certain time in their life. I was lucky to have THE FRONT ROW SEAT to this revelation.

Now it's your turn to take a front row seat in YOUR life! Ignite our movement to celebrate everyday champions by answering these two calls to action.

1. **Identify and thank those who have helped you! Use the tools I have provided in the book.**
2. **Stop, look around and see whose life you can ignite!**

To help you take the first step, use the tools provided in the following pages. Complete the quick activity that will guide you to identify and remember the one(s) who believed in you. Then, reach out today and thank, honor, and/or acknowledge that special "one" with some words of appreciation. They'll be so glad you did!

Call to Action Tools

Who has believed in you?

Here is a way to delve deeper into your personal story. I call it I.T.P. (Identify, Thank, Pass It on)

- **Identify:** I encourage you to spend quality and thoughtful time while you are freshly inspired by these amazing stories. Use the "OWB Worksheet Grid" to write down the names of your influencers. Next, write down your memories, and even create a story of your own using the "OWB Questionnaire" on the following page.

- **Thank:** Act swiftly and with gratitude. There are so many ways to say thanks! Take the time today -- while you have it -- while you are freshly inspired by your own story. Here are a few ways to show your gratitude:

    1. I have included a thank you note template as a reference to help you get started.

    2. Visit our website. Cut and paste our logo and #OWB Seal of Approval to attach to your note on Facebook, LinkedIn, Twitter, or Email to the one(s) who believed.

    3. Call them, take them to lunch or dinner. They would love to know how much you appreciated their support. They would love to know how their goodwill to you has benefited others.

- **Pass It On:** Live intentionally and pass on the legacy of the human spirit! I encourage you to act from a mindset of purpose, sincerity, giving (not receiving) and with increased awareness. Live in the moment with increased self-awareness. If someone needs a hand, offer it. Become a volunteer or a mentor. Create a scholarship if you are financially able or create other ways to spread goodwill if you are not.

Now It's Your Turn

Use this OWB Worksheet Grid to brainstorm the names of people who have believed in you.

Family/Friends	*School/Education/Sports*
Work/Career/Business	*Other (Church, Stranger, Hero)*

The Ones Who Believed Questionnaire

Dive deeper into your stories with this thought-provoking OWB Questionnaire. Five are provided, but feel free to make as many copies as you need!

Name of person: _____

Where did you meet? _____
_____
_____
_____
_____

How did he or she positively influence and shape the direction of your life? Go into detail, remember the event or specific memory that defined their belief and support.

_____
_____
_____
_____
_____
_____
_____
_____
_____
_____
_____

How did their support impact your life? How did it make you feel? Be specific! _____

_____
_____
_____
_____

How did their support or belief in you impact the lives of those around you?

_____
_____
_____
_____

Do they know how grateful you are?

What do you think they would say once you thanked them?

_____
_____
_____
_____

Jot down your initial thoughts about what you'd like to say to them: _____

_____
_____
_____
_____

The Ones Who Believed Questionnaire

Dive deeper into your stories with this thought-provoking OWB Questionnaire. Five are provided, but feel free to make as many copies as you need!

Name of person: _____
_____

Where did you meet? _____
_____
_____
_____
_____
_____

How did he or she positively influence and shape the direction of your life? Go into detail, remember the event or specific memory that defined their belief and support.

_____
_____
_____
_____
_____
_____
_____
_____
_____
_____

How did their support impact your life? How did it make you feel? Be specific! _____
_____
_____
_____

How did their support or belief in you impact the lives of those around you?
_____
_____
_____
_____

Do they know how grateful you are?

What do you think they would say once you thanked them?
_____
_____
_____
_____

Jot down your initial thoughts about what you'd like to say to them:
_____
_____
_____
_____

The Ones Who Believed Questionnaire

Dive deeper into your stories with this thought-provoking OWB Questionnaire. Five are provided, but feel free to make as many copies as you need!

Name of person: _____

_____
_____
_____
_____

Where did you meet? _____

_____
_____
_____
_____

How did he or she positively influence and shape the direction of your life? Go into detail, remember the event or specific memory that defined their belief and support.

_____
_____
_____
_____
_____
_____
_____
_____
_____
_____

How did their support impact your life? How did it make you feel? Be specific!

___

How did their support or belief in you impact the lives of those around you?

___

Do they know how grateful you are?

What do you think they would say once you thanked them?

___

Jot down your initial thoughts about what you'd like to say to them: _____

___

The Ones Who Believed Questionnaire

Dive deeper into your stories with this thought-provoking OWB Questionnaire. Five are provided, but feel free to make as many copies as you need!

Name of person: _____
_____

Where did you meet? _____
_____
_____
_____
_____

How did he or she positively influence and shape the direction of your life? Go into detail, remember the event or specific memory that defined their belief and support.

_____
_____
_____
_____
_____
_____
_____
_____
_____
_____
_____

How did their support impact your life? How did it make you feel? Be specific! _____
_____
_____
_____

How did their support or belief in you impact the lives of those around you?
_____
_____
_____
_____

Do they know how grateful you are?

What do you think they would say once you thanked them?
_____
_____
_____
_____

Jot down your initial thoughts about what you'd like to say to them: _____
_____
_____
_____

The Ones Who Believed Questionnaire

Dive deeper into your stories with this thought-provoking OWB Questionnaire. Five are provided, but feel free to make as many copies as you need!

Name of person:_____
_____

Where did you meet?_____
_____
_____
_____

How did he or she positively influence and shape the direction of your life? Go into detail, remember the event or specific memory that defined their belief and support.

_____
_____
_____
_____
_____
_____
_____
_____
_____
_____
_____
_____

How did their support impact your life? How did it make you feel? Be specific!_____
_____
_____
_____

How did their support or belief in you impact the lives of those around you?
_____
_____
_____
_____

Do they know how grateful you are?

What do you think they would say once you thanked them?
_____
_____
_____
_____

Jot down your initial thoughts about what you'd like to say to them:
_____
_____
_____
_____

Sample Note of Thanks

Feel free to use the following template as a basis for reaching out to the person you want to thank.

Dear _____ (first name),

I just finished reading a book titled *The Ones Who Believed: True Inspirational Stories Honoring Everyday People Who Took a Chance, Shaped a Life and Made a Difference*. The stories in it made me think of you and inspired me to send this note of thanks.

    Back when we/During the time in my life when I was _____ _____ (insert the circumstances of the situation you are recalling), you helped/taught/inspired/influenced/made an impact on me, and I have never forgotten it.

    You helped me to overcome/see/believe/understand/figure out _____ _____ (insert description of what your one helped you do -- for example, "understand myself in a way no one else could" or "see my potential for graphic design" or "overcome the hardships of my childhood"). Because of you, I now _____ (insert description of the result their influence had on you -- for example, "am a teacher" or "run a successful business" or "am happily married to the man/woman of my dreams" or "donate 5% of my company's profits to this charity").

    As I've grown older, I've come to appreciate the people in my life who have been there for me in one way or another. I didn't want to go another day without letting you know how much you mean to me.

Sincerely/Warmly/Best,

Your Name

(optional -- contact info or include your business card if mailing a sealed envelope)

Mentoring's Powerful Legacy

rippler (n) someone who effects a positive change in another's life that has far-reaching and long-lasting impact.

Mentoring is a popular topic these days given our accelerated, dynamic business climate. Established company and organizational leaders around the world consistently look for ways to develop their talent and shape their employee succession plans. Mentoring is considered an essential leadership tool to achieve these goals. In addition to managing and motivating people, it's also important to consider how we can each help others learn, grow and become more effective in their jobs. A quick Internet search yields countless articles on designing, developing, maintaining, and evaluating formal, corporate mentoring programs. Some readers of this book may even be in a position within a company or organization that manages such programs, and I applaud your efforts to help others advance personally and professionally.

Other readers may be interested in either becoming a mentor or being mentored. *Am I continuing to learn and grow?* is a question several people asked in the preceding stories. It is a question I asked myself when I accepted the personal challenge to write this book, and I have, indeed, learned many things. This question gets at the heart of what mentoring is all about. Throughout the different seasons of our lives, we are all both teachers and learners – whether we realize it or not. At various points, we are the teacher, the student, or both simultaneously. This is the beauty of the human experience.

While I didn't set out to write a book about mentoring, many of the stories provide fascinating insights into not only the power of the mentoring experience, but also to the powerful influence of those organic, informal relationships I referred to in the Introduction, what I call "ripplers." It is true that the two experiences share certain qualities, and both provide value to the people involved, but one significant characteristic makes them different: the experience's *source*.

A traditional, formal mentoring relationship is often prescribed with a conscious approach from the outside in, whereas *the rippler relationships that evolve organically from an unseen but potent force* come from the inside-out, much like ripples in a pond form when something from below the surface rises. Gaining this deeper understanding of what makes mentoring relationships successful was one of the many surprises of this project.

Mentoring, it turns out, is not rocket science. It doesn't come with a set of operating instructions everyone can follow and achieve the same results. Most of those interviewed for this book did not partake in a formal program or training; there was simply a learning community and a climate of trust that fostered their growth.

For example, many parents and grandparents in this book were recognized for not only their belief in someone else, but also for the loving foundation they laid for their families (our first learning community). They gave great advice and lived by it. They led by example and inspired their children to do the same. This became their living legacy, one that will likely get passed on and ripple through generations to come. Robert Hayman's story, "Nothing but the Best," is an excellent example of this concept in action.

Other interviewees discovered they were unwitting recipients of a mentoring experience and described their mentors as parent figures. They related stories of how the ones who believed stepped in and guided them along uncertain paths for their own parents or filled the void for absent or departed parents. These interviewees were often unaware of the powerful influence they were under. The relationships demonstrated that mentorship does not always start in the home and that personal success is not dependent upon a healthy home environment and can, indeed, happen in spite of it.

The ones who believed also emerged from elementary and post-secondary learning communities. Teachers and professors cultivated environments conducive to personal discovery and unearthed hidden talents and passions. They took a selfless interest in their pupils who, in several stories, reinvested in others by becoming educators, coaches, and philanthropists.

Other mentors played significant roles in business and career success. They extended a hand to someone who reached out and asked for it, or to someone who needed to be uplifted and didn't. These business leaders either mined or polished a diamond in the rough. They helped another person overcome anxieties and fear, sharing their knowledge and wisdom to help them achieve their full potential. These leaders encouraged them to accept new challenges and reach beyond their current roles and capabilities. This belief in another person precipitated positive changes, which generated even more opportunity. They were catalysts in our interviewees' lives, propelling them forward by encouraging greatness and innovation or, in Bibop Gresta's experience, disruption.

Just as many of the interviewees were unaware of the powerful influence they were under that would forever change their lives, I suspect that many of those honored in this book were also unaware of the powerful influence they were exerting at the time. Rather, they had simply decided to be present in someone's life and to nourish that relationship. They were the parents who turned off their cell phones to share a family dinner. They were the grandparents who were doing the right thing before their grandchildren had figured out what that meant. They were the teachers who validated a student's opinion. The colleague who showed compassion and eased a struggle. They were all ones who believed and that belief was unscripted. This is the most natural, sustainable type of rippler—the one with invisible footprints.

Given these insights about mentoring's powerful legacy, what, then, are some best practices we can adopt regarding mentoring in our own lives?

First of all, it's important to remember that mentoring is about giving the gift of time and presence in someone's life, not about reaping recognition or credit for your efforts. True engagement with another requires actively listening to what they are saying, and responding in a way that shows they have been heard. If you choose to reinvest in others, do so with the intention of giving, not receiving. Give from a place of sincerity, the heart, with an "other" mindset to truly understand what others are going through. A genuine sense of "otherness" is so powerful and underestimated at times! Mentors act as a guide, offering advice and support. They are willing to accept that the mentee may not follow their advice and/or make a misstep along the way. Regardless of inevitable obstacles, both teacher and student should recognize that mistakes present opportunities to learn, grow and succeed.

Secondly, if someone approaches you for mentoring, receive their request graciously. People often know what they need in a mentor and actively seek out those qualities or skills in another. If a better fit for them exists elsewhere, point them confidently in the right direction rather than try to manufacture or prescribe a personal connection or meaningful relationship that may feel unnatural or forced. A good match exists somewhere!

Also recognize that proper timing is important. As Jim Estrada pointed out in his story "Success Has Many Parents," "Mentoring is a personal decision that should be passed on when the time is best for maximum impact." Just don't let a perceived lack of time create a barrier to forming personal connections with others and participating in this fulfilling relationship.

If you are to have a good relationship with a mentor, it's important to understand how to make the most of the relationship. Committed participants show initiative, and they recognize that achieving their goals can happen much faster as a result of seeking out a mentoring relationship. They surround themselves with several people at once who are at the top of their game to maximize the experience. Like good mentors, students must also be active listeners who are truly present in the moment and are open to input. If they are, they will receive the right messages at the right time. They must recognize that they don't have all the answers and be receptive to learning from the experiences of others. They are willing to consider new ways of thinking, to try new things, and take risks for the sake of their personal and professional growth.

Finally, even if you haven't yet experienced *one who believed* in you, don't let that stop you from becoming the person who believes in others! You can be the one who takes an interest in, brightens, or jumpstarts another's future even if you haven't benefited from the experience yourself. Winston Churchill once said, "Attitude is a little thing that makes a big difference." As we have seen from the stories, mentorship is a two-way street and requires commitment and a positive attitude from both parties. When you reflect on the deeply personal experiences shared in this book, you will see that this couldn't be more true.

Reinvesting the rewards we've received from the rippler relationship can be one of the most gratifying experiences of our lives. Debbie Johnston illustrated this concept beautifully in "A Soft Landing" when she said, "I believe when we get to the top of the elevator of life, it's our job to go back down and get the next person." This reinvestment not only directly enriches the lives of both the mentor and the person who benefits from their influence, but it also peripherally affects and benefits those around them. Everyone is lifted up. How powerful these relationships are and how expansive the breadth of their collective influence!

But most importantly, as I mentioned in the introduction, one undercurrent that flowed through all of these stories is that *the ones who believed* taught the interviewees to believe in themselves. They gave them the self-confidence to rise above self-limiting beliefs and boosted their self-esteem, making their goals seem more achievable. Believing in yourself is the most important factor in achieving personal and professional success. Others may believe in and support you through a difficult or vulnerable time, but ultimately, you must have the courage and confidence to face life's challenges on your own.

When you think about it, almost everything you do has some effect on someone else. Their reaction will, in turn, affect others. The ripple effect in action creates immeasurable ripples, and these ripples collide and take on a life of their own. *Drop a "pebble" of belief in someone's life* and imagine the impression it will leave on them, their children, their grandchildren, their communities. Ultimately, ripples return to their origin. Be remembered for the lives you positively impacted. When it's time to reflect on your life and the impression you made, those you believed in will be one of the most significant and cherished parts of your legacy.

Afterword

An Invitation from Karen Lopez McWilliams

I want to hear from you!

A big part of my mission is bringing to light the universal connection between belief and success, that "Golden Thread" several storytellers highlighted as they remembered the ones who believed and made a difference in their lives.

Will you become a part of our global movement?

There are so many amazing stories of ones who believed. I'd love for you to share yours with me and the OWB community as we continue to grow and expand our vision.

Visit us at www.OnesWhoBelieved.com to learn more, share your stories, and find other useful resources! Learn how we can prepare your story as a gift for someone special in your life.

Get Social with OWB!

Acknowledge someone who believed in you and engage your audience by tagging your person in your posts and using any or all of the following hashtags:

#OWB
#legacy
#mentoring
#rippleeffect
#OWBRippler

Helpful Internet Resources

Finding people in the digital age is easier than ever. Here are some popular ways of finding those connections from your past:

LinkedIn: www.linkedin.com

Twitter: www.twitter.com

Facebook: www.facebook.com

Find Your Ancestors: www.ancestry.com

Online Phone Book: www.anywho.com

Switchboard: www.switchboard.com

Google News Search (over 200 years of info here): www.news.google.com/news/advanced_news_search

U.S. News Archives: www.ibiblio.org/slanews/internet/archives.html

Yahoo Free People Search: www.people.yahoo.com

Your Family: www.yourfamily.com

Census Finder: www.censusfinder.com

Family Search: www.familysearch.org

Zoom Info: www.zoominfo.com

Key Questions for Group Discussion

Use the following list of questions to spark a discussion with your book group, work team, organization, or family the next time you gather around the dinner table.

1. What is the universal connection between belief and success?

2. How do the ones who believe affect the seasons of our lives?

3. In what ways do others influence who we become?

4. What are the best ways to thank those who have believed in us?

5. How is the belief we experience from someone at work the same as the belief we experience from someone at school? How is it different?

6. Does mentorship have to be formal to be effective? Why or why not?

7. Which story(ies) really spoke to you? What made it(them) stand out?

8. What is the "golden thread" that connects you to someone who believed in you?

9. How have you changed from reading these stories?

10. How can you challenge yourself to leave a legacy embodying the concept of "The Ones Who Believed"?

11. In what specific ways could you see yourself supporting the #OWB Movement?

Key Questions for Personal Reflection

The following questions from each of the stories are designed for you. Use them as a springboard for writing in your journal, discussing them with others or simply quietly thinking about what they mean to you.

1. When was the first time you began to believe in yourself?

2. As we discovered in Tristan James's story, "Walking towards Greatness," overcoming self-limiting beliefs isn't easy. When did someone in your life help you overcome your self-limiting beliefs? Who was your "Mr. Hitt?" (See page 15.)

3. What was the most uplifting piece of advice you've ever received?

4. Who has been the most steady and consistent force in your life?

5. If you could create your own "Sum of 5" with anyone living or dead the way Mark Lack referenced in his story, "A Package Combo," who would they be and why? (See page 47.)

6. From your vantage point, what specific qualities make a mentoring relationship magical?

7. Think about a time when the power of others fueled your own aspirations and you were able to accelerate your career, goals, or life forward.

8. Who have you known – either personally or observed from a distance – that is a "rock steady, leveling, positive force?" the way Shirley Palmer was for Krista in "The Ride through Two Worlds." What have they done specifically that you would want to model? (See page 87.)

9. How has a profound experience in your life helped you discover your purpose and, in turn, make a difference to others?

10. What's one overarching goal you'd like to achieve to make your American Dream come true?

11. Who has been a good listener in your life? Do you consider yourself a good listener? Why or why not?

12. What is your measuring stick for success? (See page 39.)

13. What is your motto? What words do you live your life by?

14. Think about someone in your life who could be going through something difficult "behind closed doors" the way Nicole Gibson did with her mom. How could you reach out to them and brighten their day? (See page 123.)

15. What will be *your* legacy?

16. As Newy Scruggs suggests in his story, "The Power of Impact," we all need to ask ourselves questions from time to time about our lives. When was the last time you asked yourself: *why am I doing what I'm doing?* (See page 139.)

17. Maya Angelou's quote is very powerful: "People will forget what you said, but they will never forget how you made them feel." Who in your life comes to mind when you think of this important quote?

18. How can you reach out and help someone get back on track with their life?

19. What positive lessons have you learned from your failures as an entrepreneur (or employee) to become successful today?

Key Questions for Personal Reflection

20. Take a moment and think about someone who may have gone to bat for you the way Mary Lou Kayser's teacher did for her in "The Golden Thesaurus." When have you done that for someone else? What was the outcome? (See page 167.)

21. What path did you take that was different from what was expected? How did it work out for you?

22. Describe a time when you used hard work, passion and grace to move past something that went wrong like Eddie did in "One Hot Night." How did this experience impact you? (See page 181.)

23. How have your perceptions of a person of influence in your life changed over the years?

Contributor Profiles

Brad Ball

Brad Ball should have become a doctor or a priest given his family heritage. Instead, he opted for advertising as the perfect blend between movies, television, and business. Before graduating college, Brad joined a local retail agency – which opened his eyes to the advertising world. He eventually got his name on the door at Davis, Ball & Colombatto Advertising. He has worked with global brands including McDonald's, Warner Bros., and NASCAR. Most recently, the original, indoor trampoline park, Sky Zone, brought Brad in to drive global growth and dominance worldwide. Brad and his family are native Californians, living in San Marino.

Lisa Deer

Lisa Deer has twenty years of experience in autism programming, from early childhood intervention through young adult support. She is passionate about facilitating better educational, career and residential opportunities for individuals with autism, as well as providing support and training to increase well-being and foster independence. Lisa is currently pursuing her master's degree in interdisciplinary studies and working toward her credential as a Board Certified Behavior Analyst. She lives with her family in North Richland Hills, Texas.

Dr. Bill Dorfman

Dr. Bill Dorfman is not just a famous cosmetic dentist; he is *the* famous cosmetic dentist. Affectionately known as "America's Dentist," Dr. Bill is widely recognized worldwide as a leading dentist who is responsible for creating smiles for many of Hollywood's brightest stars. He has starred on the hit ABC series *Extreme Makeover* as well as been the number one guest co-host on the syndicated daytime talk show, *The Doctors*. In addition, Dr. Dorfman is a world-renowned lecturer and author of the best-selling cosmetic dentistry book, *The Smile Guide,* and the NY Times bestseller

Billion Dollar Smile. Dr. Bill Dorfman has been interviewed extensively for numerous magazines and television shows including ABC's *Good Morning America*, *The View*, *Oprah*, CNN's *Larry King Live*, NBC's *The Today Show*, *The Tonight Show with Jay Leno*, *Dr. Phil*, *The Rachael Ray Show*, *The Tyra Banks Show*, and *Entertainment Tonight*.

John Lee Dumas

John Lee Dumas is the founder and host of *EOFire*, an award-winning podcast where he interviews today's most successful entrepreneurs seven days a week. JLD has interviewed over 1200 entrepreneurs and *EOFire* generates over 1 million monthly listeners. John's latest project is *The Freedom Journal*, a gorgeous, leather-bound journal that guides you in accomplishing your #1 goal in 100 days. Launched on Kickstarter, it raised $453k in 33 days and became the #6 most funded publishing project of all time.

Jim Estrada

Jim Estrada is a nationally renowned expert in marketing communications with over 30 years of advertising and public relations experience. The southern California native founded Estrada Communications Group in San Antonio, Texas, in 1992. Based in Austin, Texas, he has counseled many of the nation's most renowned corporations and public/nonprofit clients and provides strategic counsel related to the Hispanic Consumer Market (HCM) and ethnic community/media outreach across the USA. He has worked with global brands including Anheuser-Busch, Inc. and McDonald's. His award-winning book, *The ABCs and Ñ of America's Cultural Evolution: A Primer on the Growing Influence of Hispanics, Latinos, and Mestizos in the USA* (Tate Publishing, 2013), is available at book retailers across the nation. Personalized, signed, "collector" hardcover and paperback versions of the book are available through the author's website.

Nicole Gibson

Autrana Nicole Gibson was born and raised in Fort Worth, Texas. For the past twenty-one years, she has had a very exciting and successful career with McDonald's. She has been recognized with multiple awards for her contributions, including the "Outstanding Supervisor" award several years running. Currently, she supervises five restaurants and enjoys working with customers and staff. Nicole is committed to living her best life and creating memories with very close friends and family. Outside of work, she enjoys reading, organizing people's homes, and learning about the lives of others and what matters most to them.

Eddie Gossage

Eddie Gossage is the President of Texas Motor Speedway, one of the largest sports facilities in North America. He has been recognized as one of the more innovative speedway managers in motorsports today. A native of Nashville, Tennessee, Eddie has been involved in motorsports since 1980. His varied experiences in all major forms of auto racing have made him one of the most influential executives in professional sports. Under Eddie's leadership, Texas Motor Speedway staged the first-ever, nighttime IndyCar Series race, and hosted the largest crowd in Texas sports history. He serves on the board of directors for Speedway Children's Charity, for the Fort Worth Chamber of Commerce, and the Fort Worth Convention & Visitors Bureau. Eddie resides in the Dallas-Fort Worth area.

Bibop Gresta

Bibop Gresta is considered an expert in finance, transportation and media, specializing in mass market communications and building and project designs. He is a world-renowned speaker and serves on the boards of several humanitarian projects. His work spans the decades and includes stints in the music and entertainment industries, entrepreneurship, and hi tech. Today, Bibop serves as the CEO and co-founder of Jump Starter, Inc. and is the chairman and COO for Hyperloop Transportation Technologies, Inc. He coordinates a team of 450 engineers in 21 countries, which is currently building the first Hyperloop.

Dr. Robin Hall

Dr. Robin Hall is a board certified family physician who has been practicing medicine in the Colleyville/Southlake area of Texas since 1991. She graduated magna cum laude from Texas Wesleyan University in Fort Worth with a Bachelor of Science degree in biology and a minor in business. Dr. Hall received her Doctor of Osteopathic Medicine degree from The University of North Texas Health Science Center/Texas College of Osteopathic Medicine in Fort Worth. Following her residency, she became board certified by the American Osteopathic Board of Family Medicine. Dr. Hall lives in the Dallas-Fort Worth area of Texas with her husband.

Robert Hayman

Robert Hayman is a highly motivated, well-trained and world-class entrepreneur and the Chief Executive Officer of Hayman Properties, LLC. A seasoned entrepreneur, Robert has led corporations through market expansion, new product development and organization of transformational efforts. Outside of the real estate paradigm, Mr. Hayman's prior experience also includes executive management positions with Giorgio Beverly Hills Fragrance in New York, London and Beverly Hills. He has served on many boards and currently serves on the Board of Alphaeon (a division of Strathspey Crown) and the Malibu Chamber of Commerce. Mr. Hayman received his bachelor's degree in business administration from Boston University and pursued his master's degree in psychology at Pepperdine University, with studies also at The Sorbonne University in Paris, France.

Tristan James

Tristan James used to be your average teenager who was great at only two things: eating junk food and playing video games. That all changed at age 15 when Tristan and his family experienced two personal tragedies. Since then, he has become an expert in human motivation, which led him to receiving endorsements from Pastor Joel Osteen, Mike Tyson, Olympic gold medalists and more. Currently, he is the youngest, international life coach in the industry of personal development, a bestselling author, and a nationally recognized motivational speaker. He has shared the same stage with Paula Abdul, Michael Strahan, Apolo Ohno and more. Tristan currently attends Virginia Commonwealth University and is studying mass communication. His book, *The Water Hose*, contains techniques he used to untangle his life.

Debbie Johnston

Debbie Johnston is an entrepreneur known for starting a compassionate home health care company called Care Advantage. Recognized throughout the Richmond, Virginia, area and across the state of Virginia for public speaking, seminars, and workshops for home health, nursing, starting a business, philanthropy, and prosperity mentoring, Debbie works with a wide variety of people to help them achieve their goals. Also known for giving over a million dollars to local charities, nonprofits, organizations, and individuals in the community, as well as being featured on ABC's reality TV show, Secret Millionaire, she donates her time and resources to causes she believes in.

Katherine Jones

Kathie Jones is a Life and Recovery Coach currently living and working in Vancouver, WA. She has more than four decades of helping others help themselves to gain real-world and business experience. She earned her associate's degree and certification as a Paralegal in 1988 from Southern Methodist University, and her Coaching Certification in 2013 through the Gardner Institute in Dallas, Texas. She spent 20 years of her career working as an Environmental Paralegal traveling throughout the United States, Europe and Australia. Today, Kathie offers a wide range of coaching services for individuals and groups, as well as seminars and keynote speeches.

Mary Lou Kayser

Mary Lou Kayser is an author-entrepreneur, ghostwriter, business strategist, and speaker dedicated to helping people use writing and storytelling to lead extraordinary lives. She is the founder and CEO of The Kingfisher Group and host of the *Play Your Position* podcast, a show that celebrates leadership, achievement, and mastery. Her book, *Personal Branding Secrets for Beginners,* has become a go-to read for thousands of professionals worldwide. Mary Lou earned her bachelor's degree in English from the University of Puget Sound and her master's degree in teaching from Lewis and Clark College. She lives with her family on the edge of Oregon wine country and dreams of taking her two children on a kayaking adventure in Greenland someday.

Mark Lack

Mark A. Lack is the founder and CEO of Shorten the Gap. He is also the host of Business Rockstars, which is the number one radio/TV show for entrepreneurs, as well as the President of the Ultimate Game of Life. Mark sits on the board of trustees at The Center for Integral Wisdom, and on the board of advisors for The LEAP foundation, which is the world's #1 youth motivational leadership program for young adults aged 15-24. He is the author of the best-selling book, *Shorten the Gap: Shortcuts to Success and Happiness.* Mark lives in Long Beach, California.

John Lopez

John Lopez is co-founder (with his wife Pat) and managing partner of Sueños, LLC in Oklahoma City, Oklahoma, as well as the founder and chairman emeritus of Lopez Foods, Inc. John has been recognized with multiple awards for his outstanding business achievements and contributions to the community, including Entrepreneur of the Year in 2002 by *Hispanic Business Magazine* and the 2011 Full Service Hotel of the Year by *Latino Hotel Association's Estrella Awards.* Outside of running businesses, John has been involved over the years with several boards such as the Latino Hotel and Restaurant Association, Smithsonian Latino Center and Jim Thorpe/NFL Players Ronald McDonald Golf Classic. John has been happily married to his wife Pat for 57 years, and is the proud father of five entrepreneurial children and 22 grandchildren, including five great grandchildren.

Bryant McKeon

Bryant McKeon is a student, avid traveler, and volunteer. Born and raised in Keller, Texas, for eighteen years, he is now serving with Americorps FEMACORPS. After graduating a semester early from Keller High School, he began his 10 months of service in California and has since worked disaster relief for Louisiana and West Virginia. He is currently working in Washington D.C. at FEMA headquarters on a variety of projects from web design to writing policy. Bryant plans to attend college in the fall of 2017 and graduate with a degree in film production and business management.

Karen Lopez McWilliams

Karen Lopez McWilliams was born and raised in Glendale, Arizona, and started working at age 14 when she helped her parents open their first McDonald's restaurant in downtown Los Angeles. As a swing manager, she learned the ins and outs of the business and formed her strong work ethic. After attending Citrus Community College and then graduating from California State University of Fullerton, Karen married her soulmate, Chalmer McWilliams III. In 1993, they became approved McDonald's operators and moved to Texas to open their first franchise. Since then, Karen, Chalmer and their team have been recognized with multiple awards for their outstanding contributions and for giving back to their communities. In 2004 Karen and Chalmer received the prestigious Golden Arch Award, which is the highest honor a franchisee can achieve on a global platform. In her spare time, one of her hobbies is Mindset for Success coaching, which gave way to *The Ones Who Believed* passion project. The book is now inspiring a global movement for people to thank the one(s) who believed in them. Karen lives in the Dallas-Fort Worth area of Texas with her husband, son and daughter. Let's not forget their two dogs, Ginger and Mickey, and Rosie the cat.

Ben Osario

Ben Osario is an entrepreneur who resides in Texas. He's married to Elaine and has three beautiful daughters.

Melissa Nickelson

Melissa lives in Fort Worth, Texas, and is a proud Texas girl. She lives with her husband, Gary, a family law attorney, her son, and two slightly spoiled dogs. Melissa was a family law legal assistant for 17 years before becoming a life coach and a certified divorce coach. Melissa works with clients individually and in group sessions to help others work through the pain and emotional side of divorce. She is the author of *From Mrs. To Ms: A Guide to Living Your Life During and After Divor*ce. Melissa is fond of chocolate, shoe shopping, reading, traveling and exploring new places and is always up for a new adventure, especially if laughter is involved. Her motto in life is: "Choose Happy! Happiness is a choice."

Krista Dabakis Price

Krista Dabakis Price is an educator, writer and trainer who has worked for colleges and universities teaching career-related skills such as team building, goal setting, change management, communication skills, and mission statement development. Krista has more than 20 years of instructional experience and has been recognized for her excellence in the classroom with the prestigious Teacher of the Year award. She has a bachelor's degree from Washington State University and a master's degree in education from Western Washington University. Drawing on many years' experience in leadership development and classroom instruction, Krista is currently writing a book on teaching. She lives near Portland, Oregon, with her family and dog, Maya.

Johnny Rutherford
Johnny Rutherford is a man of wide interests. He won the Indianapolis 500 three times (1974, 1976 and 1980), beating Mario Andretti in 1976. He once flew his own P-51 Mustang and has said that he would like to be a fighter pilot if he wasn't in racing. In fact, his hero is General Chuck Yeager. Johnny enjoys painting, rides in celebrity cutting-horse competitions, shoots in celebrity sporting clay tournaments, and works as a television motorsports analyst. Johnny's wife, Betty, was a fixture at his side throughout his racing career and helped to end the taboo in American racing against allowing women in the pit area. Johnny, who has been invited to The White House on behalf of Indy on multiple occasions, is considered a popular ambassador and spokesman for the sport of Indy car racing. He has two grown children and lives in Fort Worth, Texas.

Newy Scruggs
Newy Scruggs is a multiple Emmy Award-winning sportscaster who has been in broadcasting since 1992. Currently, Newy is the sports director at KXAS-TV (NBC) in Dallas-Fort Worth, Texas, and is the national radio host of The Newy Scruggs Show. He graduated from the University of North Carolina at Pembroke and served on the board of trustees. The Newy Scruggs Sports Broadcasting Scholarship was established in 2003 for students who desire careers in the sports media at UNC-Pembroke. Wanting to give back to the Dallas-Fort Worth community, the Newy Scruggs Endowment for Student Enrichment Opportunities was launched at The University of Texas at Arlington in 2012. He lives in the Dallas area with his wife and children.

Julia Telligman
Julia Telligman is a professional photographer and owns a studio location in Keller, Texas. Julia has been capturing "real life" since 2000. Prior to starting her business, Julia's background was in business consulting, and she worked with multiple companies in the Dallas-Fort Worth area. Specifically, marketing and customer management were two of her areas of expertise.

To Learn More about OWB Contributors

Brad Ball
www.linkedin.com/in/brad-ball-589b033

Lisa Deer
www.linkedin.com/in/lisa-deer-b45598ab

Dr. Bill Dorfman
www.billdorfmandds.com

John Lee Dumas
www.eofire.com

Jim Estrada
http://goo.gl/FQ0KCC

Eddie Gossage
https://www.linkedin.com/in/eddie-gossage-735a778

Bibop Gresta
www.hyperlooptransp.com

Dr. Robin Hall
www.destinationhealth.com

Robert Hayman
www.haymanproperties.com

Tristan James
www.tristanjames.org

Debbie Johnston
www.debbiejohnston.com

Mary Lou Kayser
www.maryloukayser.com

Mark Lack
www.shortenthegap.com

Karen Lopez McWilliams
www.oneswhobelieved.com

Melissa Nickelson
www.MelissaNickelson.com

Krista Dabakis Price
https://www.linkedin.com/in/krista-dabakis-price-med-289a8310

Johnny Rutherford
www.johnnyrutherford.com

Newy Scruggs
www.newdawg.com

Julia Telligman
www.heritagestudios.net

About the Authors

Karen Lopez McWilliams was born and raised in Glendale, Arizona, and started working at age 14 when she helped her parents open their first McDonald's restaurant in downtown Los Angeles. As a swing manager, she learned the ins and outs of the business and formed her strong work ethic. After attending Citrus Community College and then graduating from California State University of Fullerton, Karen married her soulmate, Chalmer McWilliams III. In 1993, they became approved McDonald's operators and moved to Texas to open their first franchise. Since then, Karen, Chalmer and their team have been recognized with multiple awards for their outstanding contributions and for giving back to their communities. In 2004 Karen and Chalmer received the prestigious Golden Arch Award, which is the highest honor a franchisee can achieve on a global platform. In her spare time, one of her hobbies is Mindset for Success coaching, which gave way to *The Ones Who Believed* passion project. The book is now inspiring a global movement for people to thank the one(s) who believed in them. Karen lives in the Dallas-Fort Worth area of Texas with her husband, son and daughter. Let's not forget their two dogs, Ginger and Mickey, and Rosie the cat.

Mary Lou Kayser is an author-entrepreneur, ghostwriter, business strategist, and speaker dedicated to helping people use writing and storytelling to lead extraordinary lives. She is the founder and CEO of The Kingfisher Group and host of the *Play Your Position* podcast, a show that celebrates leadership, achievement, and mastery. Her book, *Personal Branding Secrets for Beginners,* has become a go-to read for thousands of professionals worldwide. Mary Lou earned her bachelor's degree in English from the University of Puget Sound and her master's degree in teaching from Lewis and Clark College. She lives with her family on the edge of Oregon wine country and dreams of taking her two children on a kayaking adventure in Greenland someday.

www.ingramcontent.com/pod-product-compliance
Lightning Source LLC
LaVergne TN
LVHW051546070426
835507LV00021B/2431